THE O'CASEY ENIGMA

The O'Casey Enigma

Edited by
Micheál Ó hAodha

The Thomas Davis Lecture Series
General Editor: Michael Littleton

Published in collaboration with
Radio Telefís Éireann
by
THE MERCIER PRESS
Dublin and Cork

The Mercier Press Limited
4 Bridge Street, Cork
25 Lower Abbey Street, Dublin 1

The O'Casey Enigma
First published 1980
ISBN 0 85342 637 6

Acknowledgements
Cover picture: G. A. Duncan.
Other illustrations by kind permission of The Abbey Theatre.

The Thomas Davis Lectures
General Editor: Michael Littleton.

Every autumn, winter and spring since September 1953, Radio Telefis Éireann has been broadcasting half-hour lectures, named in honour of Thomas Davis. Inspired by one of his famous sayings, 'Educate that you may be free', the aim of these lectures has been to provide in popular form what is best in Irish scholarship and the sciences.

Most of the lectures have been in series; many have been single broadcasts; some have been in English, some in Irish. In the time that has passed since they were initiated, the lectures have dealt with many aspects and with many centuries of Irish social life, history, science and literature. The lecturers, distinguished for their special learning at home and abroad, have been drawn from many nations but mainly from Ireland.

A list of the collections of Thomas Davis Lectures published by The Mercier Press is printed in the back of this book.

Printed by Litho Press & Co. Midletorn, Co Cork.

CONTENTS

INTRODUCTION

MICHEÁL Ó hAODHA

The centenary of a great Irish playwright should not only be an occasion for conventional praise and tribute but for a reassessment of his place among the major twentieth century dramatists.

Seán O'Casey in his public career was a figure of controversy and in the sixteen years since his death, no final pattern has emerged from the tangled skein of his reputed activities in such diverse organisations as a Dublin Orange Lodge, the Irish Republican Brotherhood, the St. Laurence O'Toole Pipers' Band and Conradh na Gaeilge.

These were the threads from which he wove his great tapestry of Ireland in revolution. In his talk on O'Casey and the Trade Unions, James Plunkett attributes the emergence of the mature O'Casey to the influence of Jim Larkin and the writings of Bernard Shaw, both of whom shared his disillusionment with extreme nationalism. It is a view which the biographer of James Connolly, C. Desmond Greaves, does not share. In his contribution he points out that long after O'Casey had severed his connections with the I.R.B. and the Citizen Army, he was writing propagandist verse for Sinn Féin even as late as 1918. He never claimed to be a socialist in the James Connolly tradition. One of O'Casey's blind spots, as revealed in the quasi-autobiographies, was that he could not praise his life-long hero, Larkin, without seeming to disparage Connolly, the most vital social thinker of that generation. This lack of intellectual calm is pointed out by

Brendan Kennelly in his lyrical evocation of what he calls *Seán O'Casey's Journey into Joy*.

But it is not as a political thinker or as an intellectual that O'Casey must be judged but as a dramatist. There is little point, at this stage, in praising his early Abbey trilogy. It would be something of an impertinence, and, as Brendan Behan once said, "It's like praising the Lakes of Killarney".

But this was not always the case, as Denis Johnston recalls in his reminiscences of *O'Casey in the Twenties*, when many inside and outside the Abbey were, to say the least, rather begrudging in their appreciation of his great talent. Tomás Mac Anna, who has produced most of the later plays at the new Abbey, makes a very good case for a revaluation of these works in the O'Casey canon. Hans-Georg Simmgen, who worked with the Berliner Ensemble, founded by Bertholt Brecht, writes with even greater admiration for *Purple Dust* which has been an enormous success in the German Democratic Republic.

These productions, by Hans-Georg Simmgen and Tomás Mac Anna, were notable products of what might be termed *the director's theatre*. Cyril Cusack, in a characteristic piece, attributes his own undoubted achievements as an outstanding player in O'Casey parts to the older traditions of Abbey acting which he shared with Barry Fitzgerald, F. J. McCormick and others.

The American scholar Robert Hogan tackles the more prickly problems of O'Casey's prose, with special reference to the autobiographies and critical works. But like most of the contributors to this series, he shares my view that in his plays and prose O'Casey has left us a tale told to life herself which must always have a meaning. As he once said, some of the wild joy and savage bitterness will go down into the limbo of forgotten things but much is certain to survive as an incomparable portrayal of Ireland in revolution.

O'CASEY'S TOY THEATRE

TOMÁS MAC ANNA

When talking or writing about our greatest dramatist, it seems customary to refer to the early and the later O'Casey as if there were really two separate identities under the familiar cloth cap, as if, indeed, the sudden change from the early to the later came somewhere in the middle of the Irish Sea on the boat to England, with O'Casey in the old raincoat humming "Innisfallen, Fare Thee Well" as the Dublin hills disappeared in the evening mist.

Before the *Shadow of a Gunman* O'Casey had written four plays: the script of only one of these exists and that one is *The Harvest Festival,* a roughly sketched-out sprawling piece which he later rewrote as *The Drums of Father Ned,* though there is a little of *Red Roses For Me* in it as well. One of the early four, *The Robe of Roskeen,* was published in a Republican paper called *The Plain People,* but neither the play nor the paper has come down to us. But it is the other two plays which seem the greater loss: *The Frost in the Flower* and *The Crimson in the Tricolour* which was almost produced at the Abbey. Lennox Robinson, then manager of the Theatre, mislaid the original handwritten manuscript: found it again, had it properly typed, rejected it, and then lost script and copy for all time. The title is an intriguing one, conjuring up — indeed I should say summing up — O'Casey always the patriot-socialist, and from what we know of the play, dealing with heroic socialists and villainous capitalists, black against white or, perhaps I should say black against red with no half shades between. All at once we are aware of the so-called later O'Casey, writing well before his time and place, before indeed he had a play staged at all; and I feel that I am not at all wide of the mark when one considers his second staged play — *Cathleen Listens In* which was produced at the Abbey in 1923, the same year as *Shadow of a Gunman*. The Cathleen of the title is, of course, Cathleen Ní Houlihan, rather more up to date and less of a lamenter than Yeats's Cathleen, and the short piece turns out to be a political polemical tract-for-the-times — it was just after the founding of the Free State — with all the warring factions symbolically represented before a rather confused audience, who were expecting a follow-up to the popular *Shadow of a Gunman*. O'Casey in his autobiography tells of the curtain coming down in a sort of stunned silence, but the critics seem to have accepted the piece more or less on its own terms, even if it does appear that the audience did not know just what to make of the uneasy admixture of satire, song and symbol. One could make out, I suppose, that the play was before its time, but it is also probable that the naturalistic style of the Abbey company was ill suited to the play — the Abbey was very much the Abbey then, with the best and most famous ensembles coming together — and to have the F. J. McCormick's, the Michael Dolan's and the Maureen Delaney's suddenly abandon their well established easy style to hurl themselves head-long into Pantomime and Harlequinade, for that was what *Cathleen* turned out to be, would have been, literally, a seven day wonder.

O'Casey's stage directions are colourful and exact — the tumble down houses, the colourful costumes, the tri-colour in the garden — all very similar to the setting of *Cock-a-Doodle-Dandy* thirty years later. Indeed, it is worthwhile noting that O'Casey the painter is to be found in all his stage descriptions, sometimes over-long and most elaborate. He had the eye and the

The Shadow of a Gunman
Michael F. Dolan as Tommy Owens in the first production, 12 April 1923. (Pen-drawing by Grace Plunkett.)

talent of an artist, which to the best of my knowledge he never developed — apart from odd cartoon sketches now and then — and all the scenes he describes for the theatre to realise, have in them, especially in the later pieces, the bright crayon pictures of a toy-theatre, all tuppence coloured, rather like the descriptive pieces of the same G. K. Chesterton he so often attacked, who was also something of an unpractising artist, designing toy-theatres as a hobby all his life.

In a way, when talking of O'Casey the could-be painter and that colourful exuberance which gives all his plays a singular power, capturing the stage, if sometimes eluding one on the printed page; the surprising thing is that he disciplined this exuberance—indeed this extravagance, so much in evidence in *Cathleen Listens In* — to give us the three full length realistic plays, *The Shadow of a Gunman, Juno and the Paycock* and *The Plough and the Stars*. Realistic is not quite the term to use: poetic-realistic is better, and something else not easily defined. Consider for instance the second act of *The Plough and the Stars,* the pub scene, which gathers into its theatrical image the turmoil of a whole city: the militant figure outside the window, Rosie Redmond on her bar-stool, the sudden excited comings-and-goings of shabby humanity, the entrance of the flags, the shouts and the music outside and the final bawdy song. This is an experience of total theatre that is unsurpassed on the Irish stage — possibly on any modern stage. It is no idle assumption to say that, in that magnificent act the very basis of all O'Casey, early or late, can be found. Add to that the naïve and colourful toy-theatrics of *Cathleen Listens In* and the pattern of O'Casey's tapestry, woven over the years from the rejected *Crimson in the Tricolour* to the last and still lively *Figuro in the Night* becomes clear. As it rolls on, play after play, the pattern changes, becomes brighter, at times a little gaudy, but the dominant colours remain — many shades of green, and always the orange, and finally, linking all together, the inevitable crimson.

It hardly needs to be said that *The Silver Tassie* was of first importance in O'Casey's career, but for reasons other than the famous controversy which followed the directors' rejection — and it should be remembered that both Robinson and Lady Gregory among the others, agreed with Yeats when the play finally went back.

In its admixture of styles, it represents, almost symbolically, O'Casey the poetic realist giving way to O'Casey the symbolist, and finally to the O'Casey of the music-halls. The first act, aptly enough set in a crumbling Dublin tenement, the familiar O'Casey stage-image, is a surging, singing half hour, that Yeats declared to be the best thing O'Casey ever wrote. That was before he read the second act, that powerful evocation of war, with its plaintive chants, its choruses, its mass-like — indeed, tenebrae-like — ritual.

Yeats, talking all his life about ritual in the Theatre, finding it there before him chapter and verse, colloquial it is true, bawdy perhaps, closed his mind to it, muttering something about O'Casey's lack of the actual experience of war. He might as well have sent Bertolt Brecht his *Mother Courage* back with the same complaint. True, he also added something about the change of style, and refused to make anything of the later acts with their mixture of fantasy, farce and searing tragedy, reluctant at the last to allow O'Casey to shatter their cosy theatre image, which he presided over from that musty office on Marlborough Street. Yeats was of course badly mistaken; he served the Abbey, and indeed, the Irish Theatre, badly by rejecting the play, displaying a surprising lack of imagination, and an arrogance, which ensured that O'Casey was lost to our stages for a long time afterwards, beating out play after play in a faraway limbo with no assurance of audiences at home or abroad.

After *The Silver Tassie,* O'Casey never submitted another work to the Abbey: nor did the Abbey seek one, although they were there, in print, for any theatre to try, if it had the mind to. That the Abbey did not have the mind to, first under Yeats and later under Ernest Blythe — although Blythe did open the Queens Theatre years with *The Silver Tassie* in 1951 — was the Abbey's loss and shameful neglect, even though most of the plays have now been seen there; a belated gesture when the Lion is well and truly dead.

After *The Silver Tassie* came *Within the Gates* which Dublin has yet to see in professional performance. I have often thought that it was with this play — reminiscent of the *Tassie* with its choruses and songs, but much more united in style — that O'Casey's artistic exile really began. He wrote about the play — "I am out to destroy the accepted naturalistic presentation of character, to get back to the poetic significance of drama".

He did not quite go the whole way in *Within The Gates,* nor was the conception helped by a production at the Old Royalty Theatre in Dean Street at the hands of a director, Norman McDermott, who was more at home with what O'Casey called "Noel Coward Codology" than a morality in Hyde Park. The play failed, the critics were cool when not downright abusive, but how could they have been otherwise when what they saw was a play of great symbolic power diminished to suit the milk-and-water fare of London's West End at the time? The play got a much better production in New York and was banned in Boston, but not before the New York critics — notably George Jean Nathan — had hailed its vision and originality. With *Within the Gates* O'Casey crossed his artistic Rubicon: from then on, his indulgence was in glittering words, torrents of them, and a tumbling imagery equally glittering and gay, but where was he to find, at once, a theatre, a stage and a workshop, a company, and most important of all, a director, who shared, and even fitfully realised, his exuberant vision. What O'Casey was striving for was in fact Total Theatre — that convocation of image, music, words, and verse, song and dance that means the disciplined — maybe indeed, the undisciplined — essence of the very idea of Theatre. I doubt if he ever saw this vision of his realised in his lifetime. The British Theatre had to wait many years for such a realisation: O'Casey was better served in America and on the Continent than ever he was in the occasional theatres that, from time to time, grudgingly essayed his plays. One can speak of influences here: the expressionist theatre of Germany which produced Toller and Kaiser; Maeyerhold's Theatre in Moscow; perhaps the work of Piscator in Berlin. But it always seemed to me that O'Casey in his particular vision was being true to himself, and no one else. Indeed the influences were nearer home, in the shabby old Queens in Dublin, in the teeming tenements, in his painter's eye, and undoubtedly — as he himself set down about *Within the Gates* — in the English version of the Bible and in Shakespeare. But it is true to say, as one says of Samuel Beckett and Antoinin Artaud, that he was, in his vision, and his work, completely original.

After *Within the Gates* there was a pause: he was hard at work on his autobiography, which has in it all the colourful — and theatrical — exuberance of the plays, those already written and those to come, relating to them in many not wholly unexpected ways. Next came *The Star Turns Red,* a socialist manifesto. Of all the O'Casey plays, this one became the most dismissed and the most neglected. Commentators and critics alike — with the single exception of James Agate in the Sunday Times — scorned it when it was produced by the Unity Theatre in 1946, and it must be admitted that it seems a sorry mixture in the printed text; an exercise in propaganda and little more, strident and remote in place and time. But then — and this is so true of nearly all the later O'Casey's — the play was not written to be read; it was written for the stage, even if it calls for ingenuity and not a little imagination to put it finally there. It proved so in the recent Abbey production, its abundance of riches revealed only when on stage before an audience, given that the central figure is Dublin's own Jim Larkin, and the dedication, to the Dublin workers in the infamous lock-out of 1913.

The conflict of the play is a simple one: the established power of Church and State against the downtrodden masses, not so much the similar powerful theme of Toller's *Masses and Man,* as the old time morality, indeed, basically a miracle play, with the roles of Satan and God turned upside down. It may well be that the lost *Crimson in the Tricolour* had a similar theme. I found the play on the stage surging with tremendous, almost operatic power, with something Wagnerian about it, overflowing in its emotional impact into the hushed auditorium; not Communist Dogma as some would insist, but as Seán himself was eager to point out — "the spirit and prophesy of the English Bible". One could go further and quote the "Sermon on the Mount"; "the meek shall inherit the earth . . ."

With his manifesto *The Star Turns Red,* O'Casey said a reluctant goodbye to didactic Theatre, by no means repentant; and plunged gaily into the admixture of farce and high comedy that he called *Purple Dust*. The theme is that of Shaw's *John Bull's Other Island* — the well-meaning Englishman lost in an Irish mist — although, in this instance, the other island is certainly not John Bull's and never could be. The underlying idea of the play is deadly serious. The curtain falls as the old Tudor mansion, symbol of an usurping power is swept away by the raging flood, no half-hearted symbol. But the mood is hilarious, with O'Casey indulging in scenes of farce that put him, not unexpectedly, well to the fore as a writer of that most difficult art in the Theatre, the art of farce. One recalls the daft scene where the workmen try to bring in an antique desk through a narrow window and almost wreck both house and desk in the process, and almost at once other scenes in the other plays come to mind: the workmen having similar difficulties with ladders and decorations in the Mayor's palace in *The Star Turns Red*; the two oldsters tackling a telephone in *Silver Tassie*; even the image of Uncle Peter chasing the Covey, brandishing a silly sword in the first act of *The Plough and the Stars*.

An interesting comparison here is that of Charles Chaplin. Both O'Casey and Chaplin came from mean city streets, both had a fondness for plots not far removed from the Victorian novelette, both essayed to be didactic in their later works, and it is by no means an idle endeavour to compare the early Chaplin two-reelers with O'Casey's one-act pieces, and indeed the magnificent *City Lights* with *Within the Gates*. And both revelled in the comedy of anarchy, Chaplin with mime, O'Casey with a torrent of words. In a way, these plunges into farce can be called O'Casey's trademark, sudden unexpected clowning even at the most solemn moments, as the instance in *Red Roses For Me* and *The Bishop's Bonfire*. In *Purple Dust* he shows himself at his hilarious best, although the play, when at last produced in England at the Liverpool Playhouse in 1955, proved an uneasy mixture — after all, the English audiences could hardly be expected to take kindly to the satirical English image presented, particularly after a devastating war — but it is of interest to find that Charlie Chaplin thought of it as a possible film and watched several rehearsals. Sam Wanamaker was the producer at Liverpool, but again O'Casey had failed to find the right interpreter to recreate and transform his text behind the footlights; he was much luckier in America. But then, the plays were challenging to cast and producers; it is true to say that there was nothing quite like them before and the accepted conventions just did not apply. Perhaps the worst experience O'Casey had was *Oak Leaves and Lavender* when presented at the Old Hammersmith Lyric in 1947: he wrote: "Never before had Seán seen such an assured and massive incompetency in a producer . . . a fellow who should never have been allowed even to pull up a curtain from the stage of a tuppenny gaff . . ."

This was indeed the whole problem of those later plays: to find a theatre and the Rude Mechanicals, throwbacks to a forgotten time, to wear his motley. Bertolt Brecht in exile had a similar unhappy time, but he did eventually arrive with his own ensemble, on the other side of the Berlin wall; O'Casey had no such haven. Indeed it was in the Ireland he thought to leave behind that he found true interpreters, both of them actresses; Shelah Richards, who presented *Red Roses For Me* at the Olympia in 1943 and later on, the late Ria Mooney who presented *The Silver Tassie* at the Gaiety, and in both London and Dublin the same *Red Roses For Me*. Ria once said to me that there was, to her, behind the glitter and the goings on in the plays she directed, and the others she could only wish to direct, an O'Casey cry from the heart.

My own experience of O'Casey's toy theatrics started with a small part in the Queen's *Silver Tassie*, and continued many years after as a sort of visiting consultant at the Berliner Ensemble, where Hans and Uta Simmgen were producing *Purple Dust* — a rather serious and Teutonic creation, where real water came pouring down from the wings at the final curtain. I put a script of *The Drums of Father Ned* to the Abbey Directors soon afterwards, with a note that it was our sort of play and we should do it, and back it came almost immediately with one word scrawled on the fly-leaf in Irish — "Truflais!"— which means exactly what it sounds like. Phyllis Ryan — again a well-known actress — and the Olympia management had no such reservations, and happily asked me to put the "Truflais" before a Dublin audience in 1966, who equally happily responded. It was to me a revelation to plunge at last into O'Casey's domain of many colours: we found ourselves reflected not in the dull mirror of how things are, but in a many-sided mirror, shining out as it turned and turned, with the fantasy of how things might be, should be and possibly could be. That mirrored domain is essentially O'Casey's Theatre, however tuppence coloured, a world that exists for its own sake, revealed at the rise of the curtain to have a life of its own every bit as much as Boucicault's world had a life existence, but more vibrant than ever Boucicault could imagine. Dublin had already seen that world when Tyrone Guthrie produced *The Bishop's Bonfire* for Cyril Cusack at the Gaiety in 1954 and took to it with enthusiasm, even if the critics then, as always, chorused their disapproval. To quote O'Casey again — talking of the same Cathleen Ní Houlihan that he had set to *Listening-In* so many years before "what an old snarly gob she could be at times: an ignorant one too!"

In recent years we have presented some of these later plays at the Abbey to a certain amount of success and the expected critical dissension, especially with *Cock-a-Doodle-Dandy*. Seán regarded that as his best play and, if few would agree, nevertheless his regard is understandable, as he seemed to sum up his whole life's thesis, so to speak, in this many-coloured caper, again both harlequinade and miracle play. He was in his seventies then, and angry, rather mean in his anger — in a way like Yeats in his last play *The Death of Cuchulain* — leaving us a final stage image without much hope, not a red-shirted hero in sight to pour out an ocean of words about the Utopia just over the distant hills, even if it sounded more and more like Tír-na-nÓg.

Not counting the one-acts and the hour-long pieces such as *Figuro in the Night* and *Behind the Green Curtain* — a play which has yet to find an interpreter — Seán O'Casey has given us a round dozen of major works for the Theatre, not quite as many as Brecht, and well short of Shakespeare. Taking them as a whole, one thing is at once clear, that, whether in his own native Dublin or far away in Devon or Torquay; whether in rich Dublinese or equally rich Cockney; O'Casey never really left Ireland. Indeed, even among the shades at Hyde Park or in the dripping trenches of Flanders he never left Dublin. The midland workers in *Purple Dust* are as Dublin as Fluther and Captain Boyle; the chanting soldiers of *Tassie* and the down-and-outs of Hyde Park are not that far away from Mountjoy Square. And apart from the "glitterin' words" that poured from his typewriter, characters and images echo each other from play to play. The hero figure of O'Killigain in *Purple Dust* is cousin to the messenger in *Cock-a-Doodle-Dandy* and both are kin to the Dreamer in *Within the Gates*. Michael O'Houlihan of *Cathleen Listens In* is that very same Michael Maurtraun of *Cock-a-Doodle-Dandy* and in between there was Count Religiain in *The Bishop's Bonfire*. Rory O'Balachaun of *Red Roses For Me* reappears in a more poetic light as the second workman in *Purple Dust* and there is more than a touch of Uncle Peter in that old fogey, Shanaar, in *Cock-a-Doodle-Dandy*. Saint Tremolo blowing his buccina in *The Bishop's Bonfire* has more than a nodding acquaintance with Figuro in the last O'Casey play, and the rampant dancing Cock of *Cock-a-Doodle-Dandy*. Loraleen of the same play we have seen before as Fionnuala in *Red Roses For Me*, and as the young woman, Janice, of *Within the Gates*, as well as Keelin in *The Bishop's Bonfire,* and there is a hint of Mary Boyle and Minnie Powell in all four. The orangeman Adolphus Grigson in *The Shadow of a Gunman* is not left forever in his tenement basement: we find him again well disguised as Brennan-o'-the-Moor and later still as Skerigan in *The Drums of Father Ned.*

It is as if O'Casey was weaving and reweaving the same coloured strands in different patterns, and piping out the same tunes over and over: the patriot ballads, both orange and green, the lament for a dim elegance long departed, the love songs of young and hopeful love, and the chorus of the "Red Flag" promising a new world just around the corner. There is something surreal in all this from the pen of an O'Casey whose great plays and rich characters were essentially realistic. For his messengers came in cloaks and plumed hats like the mediaeval minnesingers: his Inspector of Police in *Red Roses For Me* comes in a costume out of Ruritania; the Cock in *Cock-a-Doodle Dandy,* turns, like Yeats's silver fish into a brimming girl, and then again into a tall hat; a whole city throws off a dark and dirty cloak and becomes a New Jerusalem while the layabouts and the shawlies sing: "the drums of a never-seen Father Ned tumble a town-land upside down". This is something else again to the various Theatre movements of the century, all neatly set down and ticketed by the academicians; nothing compares to it, even if it is the very nature of Theatre itself that inspired it. It is O'Casey's very own.

Perhaps then I am near the truth when I talk of a "Toy Theatre", a thing of pleasurable manipulation, the colours worked from a child's box of crayons; indulgent if you wish, and not easy to define, and forever a challenge to both sides of the footlit stage. In a way it is a reaching back to the church-squares of the middle ages, the miracle plays with their assurance of salvation, and the rough rude companies of players, whose real merchandise was delight.

SEÁN O'CASEY IN THE TWENTIES

DENIS JOHNSTON

My association with Seán O'Casey was almost entirely confined to the Twenties, when he had only recently made a big hit in London with two of his first three plays — *Juno and the Paycock* and *The Plough and the Stars*. I was a briefless barrister at that time, living in what was called a Gents' Residential Club, while Seán, having shaken the dust of Dublin off his boots, had recently set himself up in a pleasant little flat somewhere in the West End. I forget exactly where, but it had a good address and a phone that was continually ringing with social invitations that he would have brusquely refused at home, where *Juno and the Paycock* had long been a rapturous hit while *The Plough and the Stars* had resulted in ructions.

Back in Ireland I had been one of those hangers-on in the Abbey Greenroom who are not encouraged in these days, and I remember well the early comments on the text of *The Plough and the Stars* when it first went into rehearsal. Up to that time Seán had been generally regarded as a highly successful Realist, employing the jargon and vocabulary of our city streets with great versatility, and allowing his characters to give expression to the problems of the day in a way that made most of us want to get up and cheer — sentiments that we had never heard before from the Abbey stage, even in the days of Synge.

> It's not the Gunmen that's dyin' for the People
> but the people that's dyin' for the Gunmen!

But *The Plough and the Stars* was beginning to upset some of the company by going far beyond the ordinary slang of the streets, and giving voice to sentiments on politics, and indeed on religion, that seemed to have been deliberately designed to draw sharp intakes of breath from certain quarters of the house, as well as thunderous applause from nearer the front — always the first sign of a coming storm. Not merely political objections, which, oddly enough, are not usually the first to come, but on matters of taste and morality, that are much more inflammable. For instance, there was that song, coming from the lips of a prostitute, Rosie Redmond, that ended with the lines:

> And there to our joy, a bright bouncing boy
> Was dancing a jig on the bed.

Already a member of the theatre's board of management had felt impelled to resign over some suggestiveness about this song, which he felt should be cut altogether. And there was also a word that Commandant Clitheroe took great exception to at rehearsal, when addressed by him to his wife:

> Oh well, if you're going to be snotty.

This he insisted on altering to "Oh well, if you're going to be vexed". A small amendment, you would probably think today, but having a rather peculiar effect when his wife, in reply, felt obliged to stick to the word provided in the script — "snotty". All of this sort of fuss must seem very trivial to theatre audiences of the present day, when even the Big 'F' can sometimes be heard on the Dublin stage. Indeed, we tend to forget that a great deal of O'Casey's picturesque verbiage has taken its place already in the language of the town, without much awareness of the fact that it originated with O'Casey, as, for example, "He's a darlin' man" and the use of the word "butty". But it goes further than that.

I well remember overhearing a conversation between the brothers Shields after one of the earliest rehearsals of the *Plough and the Stars,* when Barry Fitzgerald summed up O'Casey's lines by saying: "It's not like ordinary dialogue at all. It's something quite new". At which he started to recite:

> She's always dangerous and derogatory when she's well oiled. The safest way to hinder her from havin' any enjoyment out of her spite is to dip our thoughts into the fact of her bein' a female person that has moved out of the sight of ordinary sensible people.

But there were other problems that arose during the earliest readings of this very powerful work that were reported to me after I had gone to London. And so far as the old Abbey Company was concerned, they centred not only on questions of dialogue and character, but also on the author's intentions in framing his lines in a way that was peculiarly his own. In the second act of *The Plough* — the scene in the pub, which many people regard as the best piece of dramaturgy that O'Casey ever devised, there is a gorgeous bargeing match between two ladies in the play — Bessie Burgess and another dignified by the name of Mrs. Gogan in which the former says of herself — if I may quote:

> . . . Thanks be to Christ she (meaning herself) knows where she was got, and how she was got; while some she knows, decoratin' their finger with a well polished weddin' ring would be hard put to it if they were asked to show their weddin' lines!

The Plough and the Stars
Eric Gorman as Peter Flynn, M. J. Dolan as The Covey, P. J. Carolan as Fluther, Maureen Delany as Bessie Burgess and T. Moran as Corporal Stoddard. (Pen-drawing by Grace Plunkett.)

To which Mrs. Gogan replies in "a wild tempest of hysterical rage":

> Y'oul rip of a blasted liar, me weddin' ring's been well earned be twenty years be th'side o' me husband, now takin' his rest in heaven . . . an' any kid, livin' or dead, that Jinny Gogan's had since, was got between th' bordhers of th' Ten Commandments!

At this point in the first reading, one of the actresses refused to play the part at all, and it had to be given to somebody else, whereat Seán, ever kindly disposed towards his players, very decently wrote in a small new role for the offended party — that of an upper-class lady from Rathmines who had lost her way in the tumult and could find nobody to conduct her home. This character had nothing to do with the rest of the play, but was written in purely to keep a distressed lady with a part in the play. And she is still there to this day, often to the puzzlement of literary commentators who cannot see any point in her being there at all. And I may add as a comment on the later liberalisation of the Stage, that some years later the same offended player was pleased to take on the part of the whore, Rosie Redmond, without any qualms at all.

But, strangely enough, it was not to any of these disturbing passages that the audience took exception on the second night. It was when two National flags were brought into the pub by a couple of thirsty Volunteers that pandemonium broke out, and the stage was invaded by a section of a very noisy audience — mainly ladies, if I may say — and unrehearsed speeches were added to the play by both cast and public. As one of them wrote to me afterwards: "No formality at all, the audience mixing freely with the players and vice versa. Some man did his best to set the curtain on fire — a silly thing to do, because most people used to know that the old Abbey curtain was rotten with the damp owing to a leak in the roof. So nobody bothered to stop him with more serious things to attend to."

Meanwhile Yeats had been sent for from Merrion Square, and he arrived, in due course, to provide the high spot of the evening. Striding onto the stage with eyes blazing and hair awry, he shook his fist at the customers and momentarily hushed them into silence.

"You have disgraced yourselves again!" he proclaimed. "The fame of O'Casey is born tonight. This is his apotheosis."

A hush followed in the theatre, and some of the most vocal of the interrupters were seen to leave the hall — not in flight, as was afterwards explained, but in order to find out what an apotheosis was, and perhaps in the hope that it might turn out to be something irreligious, or better still, actionable. Meanwhile the play was resumed, as most of the intrusive ladies had vanished, or been pushed up the little side staircase by various members of the cast, and into the theatre's coffee bar. There they were duly found gathered around the author, Seán himself, engaged in a most genteel and amicable conversation with his supposedly hostile public — tea and cakes, in spirit at any rate, almost being handed round — some sitting on the floor beside a cosy gas fire and saying "But Mr. O'Casey, do you not feel that . . ." to which a reply would come in the soft tones of their Host and Playwright . . . "Yes, my dear young lady? Can I get you anything? What were you saying, Madam? Oh no. No sugar thank you". And so on, till the fall of the final curtain. Meanwhile, nothing more was seen of the male protestors who were still, apparently, having difficulty in finding a dictionary. Obviously it was an evening not to have missed.

On the Saturday there were, of course, two performances, and the company was not allowed to go out in the meantime as there were grave threats of kidnapping in the air. So they were accommodated with eggs and ham up in the Green Room, and a celebrated pianist called Rummel — not Rommel — called in and played classical music for them on Doc Larchet's piano. He very kindly turned up from the R.D.S. where he had been giving a recital, at the end of which he had heard that some fellow artistes were under siege in the city by hoodlums. So he set forth at once, and entertained them until it was time to get ready for the expected evening disturbance, which, in fact, did not materialise. During this very pleasant interlude the company was also visited by another of my correspondents, who reported to them the highlights of a rugby international at Lansdowne Road that he was sure they would like to hear about. ". . . The best match I've ever seen in my life. The Irish forwards were magnificent . . ." and so on.

I wonder what other city in the world could provide so many attractions and counterattractions all at the same time: a public disturbance in the National Theatre over the first production of Seán O'Casey's greatest play; a magnificent commentary by the poet Yeats; coffee and arguments with the author in the vestibule; a lively description of the best rugby international that has been seen for years, to the music of a celebrated international pianist, for the benefit of a cast under siege in its own theatre. And, finally, an evening performance to a packed house of paying public that had come notwithstanding a warning that the theatre was to be blown up. How Seán must have enjoyed all this, and how sorry I am to have missed it!

This, of course, was all before O'Casey's final departure for London, which in his autobiography he attributes to having been brusquely ordered off the Abbey stage during a scene change by Seaghan Barlow, the theatre's carpenter and oldest inhabitant. "That's why I never set foot in the place again," he explains in one of his books, regardless of the fact that the only person who hasn't been thrown off the stage by Barlow at some some or another was the redoubtable Lady Gregory, who usually carried a stick along with her usual box of Gort Cake for the company. Actually, I think it would be fairer to say that, approaching the age of forty, Seán was feeling the urge to get acquainted with a wider theatrical world than he had known down to that time. But before moving on to the few years during which I knocked around with O'Casey in his early days in London, I feel sure that some mention ought to be made of the mystery surrounding one of his earlier works that is very seldom referred to, for reasons that have never been explained.

This is a one-acter called *Nannie's Night Out,* which is set in one of those small Dublin dairies that sell sweets and toys and nick-nacks; a shop owner called Mrs. Pender has in the cast three aspiring husbands and a number of other very colourful customers, including a couple of ballad singers, a juvenile snatch-thief, an incompetent gunman, and the woman "Spunker", after whom the play is called. A spunker, by the way, is an inebriate addicted to methylated spirits as a beverage, and we are told by Robert Hogan that she was a real Dublin character known as 'Mild Millie' (a misnomer if ever there was one) with whom O'Casey is alleged to have danced in the streets in earlier days, and about whom he has-written in *Drums Under the Window.* 'Mild Millie' was a ranting roaring addict, who spent a lot of her life in jail for disturbing the peace on weekends and then going back to jail on Saturday nights for disturbing it again.

Sarah Allgood — of all people — played this part magnificently in its only Abbey production back in November, 1924. And many of those who remember it — including the saintly George Russell, and indeed myself — insist that it was a riot of a play in O'Casey's very best early style. Yet, for whatever reason, it has never been seen again, except for one production, away out in Indiana of all places, thirty-seven years later. I tried, on several occasions, to read a copy of this magnificent script, but Seán always denied that he had one. Nor was it to be found in the Abbey cupboards, which seems even more peculiar. According to Hogan, this play has had three different endings — one that Seán said he wanted, another that the Abbey preferred, and finally a compromise that has never been used. In the denoument that Seán originally wrote — but was argued out of — he has poor Nannie (as he calls her) die in the end, which of course would have spoiled the repetitive effect of into jail and out of jail and in again on the next Saturday night, that is the essence of the play's title.

Now, whether Seán was so annoyed at being cheated of a grisly ending that he suppressed the play altogether (which seems to be going rather far, even for Seán) or whether, as some allege, he intended to make use of some of his characters in a future play — which might be the answer — we will never know. But to this day, Indiana has been the only place that has been permitted to perform this masterpiece, although I am glad to say that Professor Hogan of the University of Delaware has managed to publish the text in his valuable collection of O'Caseyana, in a book called *Feathers From a Green Crow,* which I am sure can be easily obtained in New York.

But to return to O'Casey, now an international celebrity thanks to *The Plough* which was by now being produced in London. To the best of my recollection the West End Stage of 1926 could hardly be described as *avant garde* in its plays or production methods. The field of straight entertainment was, of course, largely in the hands of Mr. C. B. Cochran, who, incidentally, was one of Sean's first professional patrons so far as the stage was concerned. On the more serious side we were having a regular supply of well-constructed three-act problem plays, usually with a message. And, of course, there was the whimsey of J. M. Barrie and plenty of sexy fun from Noel Coward. Not to mention some of the later and lesser works of Shaw. Not much in any of this that was likely to be an eyeopener. But there was Chekov in Barnes, and that very remarkable Jewish play called *The Dybbuk* somewhere up near Euston, with Claud Raines in the leading part, and incidentally, a young fellow called Hilton Edwards in some small unnoticeable rôle. I remember going to this with O'Casey, and how moved he seemed to be by the visual and emotional impact that this type of production had on him. Shortly after this experience, we started going to a rather scruffy little playhouse on the upper floor of a warehouse somewhere at the back of Covent Garden, called by a name that in later years was to be used by a more celebrated group back in Dublin — the Gate Theatre. It was run by a rather hysterical director called Peter Godfrey — a friend of Hilton Edwards, who subsequently opened his Dublin experiment "in association" with Godfrey's place, and under the same name. Apart from the name, there was nothing in common between the two theatres, and as far as I know, that was the end of any so-called association.

This London Gate Theatre could hardly be described as a comfortable place as far as the public was concerned. We sat on backless benches and the ventilation left much to be desired. From somewhere to the rear of the auditorium you occasionally heard a suspicious sound of scratching and scuffles that suggested the presence of rats. But nobody minded this much — certainly not those in the front seats, to which O'Casey and I stuck determinedly, in order to get our money's worth.

The proprietor, Peter Godfrey, certainly had a wide interest and understanding of what was going on in the avant-garde little theatres of Central Europe, and he knew how to regale his public with all the new tricks of presentation that were being tried out, particularly in Germany and Russia. Non-representational dialogue, mass movement of the players, spoken choruses, short, semi-hysterical scenes, and above all, generalisation rather than characterisation — all the very opposite of the type of play that Seán had made his name with. And I think he was loving it as much as I was myself. For me it was a welcome change from the well-made three-act play — exposition, climactic action and, finally, the point! For Seán, it was a liberation from everything — from Lennox Robinson and Lady Gregory (however much she had swaddled him with her encouragement and hospitality). But above all, an answer to the unanswerable question as to what he was to turn to after his apotheosis, conferred on him by Yeats. He was just over forty, with maybe half a lifetime still to come. As a writer of genius, he had begun with *The Story of the Irish Citizen Army*. Was he to end with *The Plough and the Stars*? Never!

In those days, in the forefront of the theatre movement known as Expressionism, there were the plays of Georg Kaiser, and of a passionate little Communist called Ernst Toller who, for a few weeks in 1919, had managed to occupy the rôle of dictator of Bavaria. But not for long, because, although he could manage to write half a dozen tremendous pieces of dramatic liturgy, including *Masses and Man, Hoppla, wir leben* and *The German Hobblemann,* in which his villains were what we would regard today as broadminded liberals, he was unable to run a government, and ended his days by suicide in Brooklyn, New York. We also saw, somewhere or other, Eugene O'Neill's *All God's Chilun Got Wings,* a ponderous piece by Evreinov pretentiously called *The Life of Man*; and Capek's *The Land of Many Names*; some of which went into my own struggle with expressionism — *The Old Lady says 'No',* while Seán went on to write *The Silver*

Tassie, in which he confined the expressionist method to the second act only.

This is a very significant period in O'Casey's career, as it covers what seems to me to be a change in his outlook — a change from the natural genius of *The Plough and the Stars,* into one of international fame that begins with *The Silver Tassie,* and does not reach full maturity until it concludes with *Cock-a-Doodle-Dandy,* in which he really begins to enjoy himself again.

In the earlier stages of his career he could write in a copy of the first edition of *Juno and the Paycock:*

> To Lennox Robinson, in deep appreciation of the comradely criticism of early plays that helped the author towards a firmer and fuller dramatic expression.

But when, towards the end of the decade, he came up against the well-intentioned rejection of *The Silver Tassie* by Yeats, not out of any apparent malice, but because its expressionist second act was at that time far beyond the scope of the Abbey Theatre, he seemed to take it as a personal insult which could not be forgiven. What he wrote after the break is outside the scope of the period with which I am dealing, except to say, that with the elimination of Yeats from his dramatic hierarchy, Shaw seems to have taken his place as O'Casey's patron and firmest admirer. Whether this was a good thing or bad is not for me to say at present.

As a dyed-in-the-wool son of what we call the "North Side", O'Casey was inclined to express a certain disdain for Merrion Square and what he regarded as the middle-class suburbs of our home town, and he could seldom be tempted to parties and literary gatherings in that sort of Dublin milieu, except perhaps in one or two circles connected with the "Four

Provinces Branch". But there were other areas such as the "Friends of Soviet Union", with their fabulous collection of early Russian revolutionary posters — now somewhat dispersed, I fear — where one could meet quite a clutch of the original characters from Seán's early plays, some actually under their familiar names, who looked on him with mixed feelings on account of their unwanted fame.

But somehow in London he did not subject the local Belgravia to the obvious hostility that he applied to any signs of patronage that he felt might be coming from Ailesbury Road.

This is understandable, of course, although it was hardly fair to many of those people who, with the best of intentions tried to come to his aid when the Tassie was turned down by the Abbey. In London he was never impolite to offers of patronage, as far as I can remember, although he did not always accept it. I shall never forget his courteous evasion on the telephone to a Lady Somebody who was hoping to exhibit him at a society dinner party.

"Ah no," I overheard him explain. "You see, I've just started on another play and I have to get on with it or Cocky'll be mad. Yes'm Lady Low, it'll take me some time. There's a lot of work, you know, in writing a play. No, I couldn't say how long. Maybe the rest of the year. You never can tell. So goodbye Lady Low and thank you very much for asking me, and don't bother to ring till I call you back. It's all over my table here, and I haven't even got time for my own dinner. So good bye Lady Low, and excuse me if I ring off law garoo."

All the same he usually had time — maybe after an exhausting visit to the local "Gate"—to have a bite and a drink at some local brasserie with a fellow Dubliner like myself, and maybe with a college boy or two who would be thinking of writing a novel. London, not unlike our home town, seemed to be full of novel writers, and I remember particularly one of these just down from Oxford, who seemed to appeal to Seán in the best kind of way. And in this case Seán turned out to be right, because as a matter of fact this fellow in his later years has since become quite a celebrated and successful novelist.

Well, after a bit of preliminary banter about Oxford and the English, Seán went on to ask him his Christian name, just to loosen things up a bit.

"Well," he muttered, "I'm afraid to have to tell you that it's Rupert."

"Rupert!" says Seán. "And what's wrong with that? I've always thought Rupert a very nice name. And now I come to think of it, there's a nice street just up the road here. Rupert Street — d'ye know it? Ah I suppose not. It's full of prostitutes. Pass over your glass now and let me fill it up."

So you see O'Casey was really a very kindly person to anybody who came to him for help, and it seems to me that there was a certain amount of tragedy in the fact that he felt compelled to leave his natural home and the Abbey Theatre at so early a stage of his artistic experience, when he had found himself to be a celebrity without quite knowing why.

With a Hawthornden Prize in his pocket, Seán, understandably enough, was not conditioned to understand Yeats' perfectly good intentions and Lady Gregory's somewhat motherly sympathy, on top of Shaw's absurd pronouncement that his expressionist war scene in *The Silver Tassie* was "the finest thing ever written for the stage". So he chose to leave his natural source of material and take himself off to pastures new — the products of which are outside the dates of my present assignment. Nevertheless, we should be glad to note that before the end he left us *Cock-a-doodle Dandy* and the six volumes of a most unique autobiography.

O'CASEY AND THE ACTOR

CYRIL CUSACK

I remember — oh, those years ago that seem like yesterdays — Barry Fitzgerald, my friend and senior (he, of course, already a major part of the O'Casey scene and legend), Barry and myself in that high-up flat in Harcourt Street . . . many's the night, after some Abbey Theatre performance, talking, talking on into the dawn, talking theatre — myself sole beneficiary of so many simple stage wisdoms. Well I remember his saying, and with very solemn emphasis: "Ah, you know, once an actor starts analysing — that's the end!". In other words, that quite surely performance would then be doomed to mere mechanical mediocrity; doomed, therefore, to ultimate obscurity. And, indeed, in more recent times, alongside the play peddling the great social message, directorial over-analysis has become a weapon of destruction in theatre.

The simplest opening towards definition of O'Casey acting—circuitous perhaps—is, I would say, by way of a straight negation: there must be no pretence; or, positively speaking, it must carry reality. Acting, in its highest moments, could be described as condensed and lightning thought striking out of cloud — *from* life, *into* life — in instant communication with your audience.

Once I might have spoken of this kind of acting as being *intuitive*, but this is, after all, too easy a pronouncement. Yes, once during my juvenile days at the Abbey, in a discussion with an African university man, I argued that intuition took precedence over experience; but my black professor blandly contended that what I took to be intuition — seeing it almost as revelation — was, in fact, a babe out of the womb of experience. I think now that he may have been right.

And here I come to a point on the highway of acting O'Casey — the major signpost in fact — namely, *experience*; experience, not of theatre alone, but behind it, beneath it, back of the swinging curtain — experience of life. Nor do I argue that one must be a septuagenarian, as I am now, in order to come to that experience. In the context of O'Casey, I refer particularly to what I would call "the *Dublin* experience" which, in its city heights and depths, touches the universal. Ideally, the actor is born to it; but it may also be inherited, may even at the least be contactually communicated out of that ever-present medley of great characters continually capering, catawauling, careering about the streets of Dublin, and for all time through O'Casey's early plays — *The Shadow of a Gunman, The Plough and the Stars, Juno and the Paycock* — "the Dublin experience" indeed.

It may be expected of me, as an actor, to speak here through some of these characters as I have attempted to render them on the stage, but it would be presumptuous even to try; because, really, it is only from the stage, in true identification with the O'Casey character, that the actor may hope to know and communicate its full reality; it is only from the stage that the audience may receive it; only in that identification, that mysterious communication between actor and audience do we find mutual fulfilment — even ecstacy.

However, I think I can tell you something of how I emerged into O'Casey theatre, of certain stages of O'Casey through which I intermittently, but gratefully have passed; and, as an actor, I have happily been able to return to it.

First, I must leaf back a few pages of Abbey Theatre history. I would prefer it were actors' history, which, of course, is largely anecdotal and, I am afraid, only scantily, sometimes, indeed, scurvily served by theatre historians. For therein rests a treasure ribboned up in the memory of "the profession", or of that other archivist which is fickle and faithful by turns — our audience.

What can I do now but recite a litany of names: Sinclair, O'Donovan, Sarah Allgood, Maire O'Neill; and, fellow-founders of the Abbey Theatre, the brothers Frank and W. G. Fay; J. M. Kerrigan ("J.M." — just one of that array of tantalising initials); and Brefni O'Rorke. These were "the greats". But shall I also name the great supporting? Sidney Morgan, on whose Joxer Daly the English critic, Agate, based his elegant tribute to the supporting actor; there were Tony Quinn, Kathleen Drago, Ned Kennedy; and Harry Hutchinson, the sole survivor of that very first company, who is today a sturdy octogenarian strolling the streets of Milan.[1] Yes, these and other holy names well deserving, with the actor's leaving of the world's stage, the traditional round of applause.

A lot of fiddle-faddle is spouted out from time to time about the O'Casey "style" of acting, the Abbey "style", "ensemble playing" and so forth. I prefer to think of it rather as, say, familial acting. In other words, our theatre, despite, or because of, its many needs and small resources, with an overwhelmingly resourceful response from the playwright, provided familiar ground for mutual familiarity — with all the ties, tensions, loyalties and feuds of family — to a small society of actors.

Of so-called "ensemble" I could tell a tale or two. Take, for instance, a production of *The Plough and the Stars* at the London Embassy Theatre, over forty years ago now; the Allgood sisters not on speaking terms; O'Rorke (according to Agate, "a magnificent Fluther") and myself (the Young Covey) at purse-lipped loggerheads; then, finally, and to crown all "togetherness", Miss Allgood — Sarah — in the wings suddenly, belligerently addressing me:

"Do you think I'm fat?"

"Well . . .", I began, a little defensively, "no-o . . ."

"What, then?"

"Well, I'd say . . ." — I thought I had hit on the right word — "I'd say . . . plump!"

Just then, by the grace of God, Bessie Burgess had to make an entrance on-stage. But Miss Allgood never spoke to me again.

Yet never in that whole production was there a deliberate attempt on the part of an actor to up-stage or, worse again, down-stage another for advantage. Oh, yes . . . quite a family affair.

Having had the privilege, the pleasure and, indeed, the pain — that necessary ingredient of growth — of sharing in the work of these first Abbey Theatre actors, I believe that what this company provided, and which, essentially contributed to the making of a genuine tradition, was a strong assemblage of "stage presence". I mean "presence" as distinct from "personality", which, as often as not, is just a page torn from the gossip-column, a fake storm brewed in a paper cup; and distinct, also, from what is popularly known as "a real character" — usually no more than a public-house adornment.

From that first family of actors and the family following in greatness again — Barry Fitzgerald, F. J. McCormick, M. J. Dolan, P. J. Carolan, Denis O'Dea, Crowe — from these, still gripping hard onto the Golden Bough rather than the Golden Calf, we have received that inheritance of presence which may be called our acting tradition.

But, with all the efforts to define it, what can one say of an "acting tradition"? It, in its turn, is a racial inheritance, received and cultivated from the quality of a people — in the instance of O'Casey with an emphasis on a time of Dublin and its people. And here may I say what I think is incontrovertible; that, for O'Casey's great characters the actors require, as did the dramatist, inspiration from the special humanity of Dublin and from the sheer theatricality of Dublin life.

So, since I'm dealing primarily with acting in O'Casey, I could say that his genius had a double source of supply — not only from the life of Dublin itself, but also from a select company of Dublin actors, who were largely self-directing and who had, astonishingly, a tradition already formed from its source, the people.

At the same time, it would be wrong to suppose that our native acting was unattended by other than the Irish "presence". The Fay brothers looked rather wistfully to the French theatre, the theatre of Antoine, for technical ballast at any rate, and our actors would hardly have rejected the influence of the 500-year-old sequence of English theatre, itself by no means lost to the touch of the Irish playwright, or prevented the fluid interchange of actors between Dublin and London.

Skipping by Sheridan, Kelly, Wilde, all those exquisite charmers in theatre, it would be a failure in gratitude to ignore our indebtedness — actors and dramatists alike — to the Gardiner Street boy, Dion Boucicault. Many of our actors served their apprenticeship at the old Queen's Theatre in Great Brunswick Street, as it was, there learning the elements of "the unholy trade", and the full flavour of theatricality in Boucicault melodrama. You can see their names on the old playbills: McCormick, Craig, Fitzgerald, P. J. Carolan. Irving had acted there (Irving it was who commissioned a play from Boucicault with the simple title "Emmet!" which was, however, dropped under political pressure). There, at the Queen's, the actor could learn the technical value of exit, entrance, the grand gesture and the curtain-line, the glory of the final curtain. Yes, there was your true stage schooling.

Forgive me if I digress: is it beyond the bounds of possibility that the boy, Pearse, of 27 Great Brunswick Street, just opposite the theatre, might have taken his place in the gallery? Here also might not "a terrible beauty" have been cradled in the melodrama of the day, *Father Murphy, The Boys of Wexford, Vinegar Hill,* with actors such as Ira Allen, Roberto Lena, P. J. Bourke, Tom Moran, and those others soon to lead the way towards the shadowy waters of realistic acting on the far side of the Liffey?

Indeed, what young Irish boy then could not have been affected, fired by the heroics of melodrama! I know I was — more so, perhaps, as a child of acting parents. Through my childhood of acting in the first decades of the century there were as many as twenty companies on the road, dependent only on box-office — in a word, on the people. These were, to name but a few: O'Brien and Ireland's Co., Ira Allen's, the Carrickfords, Pat McEntee's, Dobell's, Mark Wynn's, Jack Walsh, Chalmers Mackey, and Brefni O'Rorke's Company. They served the country well. Jimmy O'Brien may yet be remembered — swinging across our rural stages, over the lake to the rescue of the Colleen Bawn. He retired from the scene at the age of ninety.

It should be remembered, too, that O'Casey once acted in Boucicault, as Father Dolan in *The Shaughraun*. Could this, I wonder, in any way have brought about, from a longing backward look, the upsurge of priests in his later plays, ending with the rebel *Drums of Father Ned*?

I would like here to include a comment from the late Gerard Fay's contribution to the souvenir programme for *The Bishop's Bonfire,* O'Casey's penultimate play, at its first production at the Gaiety Theatre in 1953:

"One of the pictures in Seán O'Casey's hallway is of himself playing Father Dolan at short notice in a production of *The Shaughraun* at the Mechanics' Theatre. Apart from the fact that the Mechanics' became the Abbey, and O'Casey one of its two greatest dramatists, I think there is another significance to this anecdote. It shows that some of the strength which O'Casey brought to the Abbey was derived from an earlier tradition — at the same time native and naïve —that was once to be seen at its best on the stage of the Queen's. It is not quite true that there was no real Irish drama before the Irish Literary Theatre, the National Theatre Society and the Abbey. The Boucicault tradition was a genuine one and its thread has been woven into the finer fabric in which the Abbey and its followers are clothed."

There was similar precedent prior to the foundation of the Moscow Arts Theatre (almost simultaneously with that of the Abbey) by Stanislavsky and his fellows.

Fay's comment puts into a nutshell a point of theatre history not widely known or accepted: that O'Casey, along with many of his actors, served an apprenticeship with Dion Boucicault; and there have been genuflections towards that master of the melodrama from the O'Casey connoisseur, David Krause, and Boucicault's latest biographer, Richard Fawkes, who see in those incorrigible characters, Myles-na-gCopaleen, Shaun the Post and Con-the-Shaughraun a valid ancestry for the Fluthers, Paycocks and Playboys. You may say that this is an over-valuation, but it effectively rids us of Peter Kavanagh's far too facile dismissal of Boucicault as the originator of that travesty contemptuously termed "the stage-Irishman" — a term which, to my mind, should be abolished and forgotten.

And now, from this "brief chronicler" a word or two of gossip, that busy exercise of idle anecdote so much a part of the tell-a-tale, make-up history of "the profession".

I came into our theatre, to turn the Shakespearean phrase, not with the big battalions but as a single spy — to watch, listen, absorb, remember; and, sharing in the work of this early generation of Abbey actors, eventually to take my place in O'Casey theatre. There they were: Sinclair the eccentric, wanting nothing so much as to top the bill in music-hall; and there the gorgeous, garrulous Allgoods; the elegant O'Donovan — spotted once staring up the stairway to the Green-room after the vanishing skirt of an aspiring actress; McCormick — "cursed", as he told me, by versatility; the lovable, easy-going, hard-drinking Carolan; the romantic Shields, who captured more than a roving eye from Synge's beloved, Maire O'Neill; Dolan — ex-British Army and stern agent of stage discipline — crabbily complaining that Protestants could not act; Protestant Fitzgerald, grand comedian in the classic mould . . . so much for "ensemble"!

Into this small family of actors I was received rather as a distant relation, in 1932. However, I came with my own private inheritance of "the Irish experience" commemorated by a grandfather stone-mason amongst the monuments of Glasnevin Cemetery, and I had my background of lengthy tours of Ireland in melodrama — all in all, acceptable credentials for later appearances in O'Casey. In time, from McCormick and Fitzgerald I had the actor's accolade of the fingered kiss into the air; then the privilege of sharing Fitzgerald's dressing-room, his ready ear, and the "gag" and giggle at my juvenile joustings with my seniors . . . "Where was I in 1916? Why, wasn't I at Mullinahone re-living eviction and the famine in the film of Knocknagow!" Above all, I could enjoy the gift of a great comedian's generous acting; I could join with him in his despisal of emasculating analysis — all a growing towards O'Casey.

I speak egotistically, yet not, I hope, in vanity; rather by way of touching on the tools of our trade —

emotion, intelligent observation, sympathetic awareness, physical presence and even a spiritual presence; in other words, the essential ingredients of life in pursuit of a totality of being. To repeat: in acting there is no room for pretence. Watching, listening, absorbing, remembering — these must be amongst the methods used towards discovery of forms of acting technique in pursuance of creative work.

I recall Barry Fitzgerald's saying to me: "I used to follow Sinclair about wherever I could find him; along the street I'd be after him, down by the quays, all over Dublin — he never knew, of course!" thus Fitzgerald, noting another remarkable actor, absorbing, studying the idiosyncracies, the cocky strut, the quirky turn of the head, never in mere mimicry — anathema to creative acting — but taking on a mantle of tradition to cast towards his great creation of the Paycock.

And time there was for listening: McCormick's reverentially irreverent stories of the Dubliner, with penetrating observation of character — no make-up needed — which the novice heard with equal reverence and relish — all converging into the classic rendering of Joxer Daly.

One cannot label McCormick with such over-used tags as "integrity", "dedication" and so on. Pure actor, his work held the chaste embrace of purity.

One of the saddest moments in my professional life was when, as a member of the audience, I came to a performance of *Juno and the Paycock* and, to my horror, Joxer was not there! McCormick had been withdrawn from the part! What a failure in recognition, and recognition of acting as an art-form — this under the aegis of a shrewd, politically-minded economic administrator, a government appointment carrying with it the theatre's first subsidy. Since then, the National Theatre Society, with a bagful of money on its back, continues its uphill struggle staggering towards full artistic recovery.

The Plough and the Stars
The late Angela Newman as Mrs. Gogan, Siobhán McKenna as Bessie Burgess, John Cavanagh as The Covey and Cyril Cusack as Fluther in Tomás Mac Anna's 1976 production at the Abbey Theatre. (Photograph by Fergus Bourke.)

Worthy of mention are the two very individual approaches to O'Casey character-finding, in my experience best represented in the work of McCormick and Fitzgerald. By this I do not mean to belittle the potential of the modern actor; but, under the depersonalising pressures of present-day society and with the intrusive influence of a form of direction, which is over-intellectualised, insensitive and alien to the acting tradition, true presence and individuality in performance are endangered, and open to being seriously diminished.

Now, as I think I have already made clear, direction in the early days of the Abbey came, not so much from without as within, in the person of the actor-director, so that, in a sense — a good sense — the actors could be said to have been self-directed. Following the Fays, Sinclair and O'Donovan (apart from Lennox Robinson, accomplished actor as well as playwright) came "inside" directors like Arthur Shields and M. J. Dolan, who were for freeing the creative spirit in theatre, but under the protection of a voluntary stage discipline.

The two differing "styles" of work in the acting of McCormick and Fitzgerald, can be outlined thus: "F.J." would identify, in total self-surrender, with the character he was portraying. He *became* Seumas Shields in *The Shadow of a Gunman*; Joxer in *Juno and the Paycock*; Clitheroe in *The Plough and the Stars*, contributing to the dramatist's originals the whole of his "Dublin experience". In this kind of acting, of course, you lose sight of the actor in the character. In contradistinction, with Barry Fitzgerald the character was absorbed into the *person* of the actor; Jackie Boyle, the Paycock, became Barry Fitzgerald; nevertheless Barry Fitzgerald was the Paycock. Which is the superior form of acting? The debate will go on, of course; but, since each was equally inspired by identification with the Dubliner, neither one, to my mind, takes precedence over the other.

I came to O'Casey in a row of smaller parts: the first, Maguire in *The Shadow of a Gunman* — Maguire typical of the time, with his bagful of bombs, a study in innocent, reckless, joyous idealism; then — most certainly one of the weaker brethren of the O'Casey family — the scarcely believable, almost unplayable Jerry Devine, whom I see as a much blackened spot of rejected Puritanism in O'Casey; again in *The Shadow of a Gunman,* the role of the Black and Tan, given extra authenticity, perhaps, by my having a Cockney mother. I would say that my graduation in O'Casey began with the Young Covey, which I patterned on a delightfully devilish young Dubliner, then on the staff of the old Theatre Royal, the house in Hawkins Street. Followed prematurely, and preferably forgotten, on Fitzgerald's departure for America, by a performance of the Paycock which, at best, was no more than a valiant recollection of the original.

I would say that my arrival — with a master's degree, as it were — in O'Casey, occurred only too recently with Fluther in *The Plough and the Stars* — Dublin, New York, Boston, Philadelphia and on to London's National Theatre, with no echoes this time of the masters, except in their echo of the inner voice of Dublin. I drew on as many as I might of the thousand and one Fluthers once abounding in this now ragamuffin city's fainting heart.

O'Casey country and its ebullient citizens are highly sensitive to reaction — in the theatrical sense. What I have not mentioned, but which may not be discounted, is the quality and effect of that most unpredictable element of theatre — the audience. In the main, for all and everywhere, O'Casey's early plays hold a common chord and capture a communication of life mysteriously beyond even that dramatist's imaginative manipulation of language. Yes, and even your Dublin audience, with its enviable disposition for taking death, and life, on a laugh, will, in the tragedies, be left, if at times a little belatedly, with some measure of bereavement.

As an actor now perhaps recovering from the glow and dazzle of yesteryears, still I find little relish in O'Casey's later plays. The rich blood of our humanity surges through the veins of those early characters, his people. With O'Casey's departure from Ireland there was a departure from the essential O'Casey as well as from O'Casey's Dublin. With him went genius working its way wordily into dramatic literature — a sprouting of feathers, a flutter of wings into fantasy across the Irish Sea. And was the poet Yeats, however arrogantly tactless, so utterly wrong?

Presumptuously, with *The Bishop's Bonfire* I thought I might repatriate O'Casey. I thought to return Dublin's dramatist to Dublin, to his roots. The sparks died fast in the hard eye of the future.

That night of *The Bishop's Bonfire* . . . it's another story, but shall I ever forget that exasperating telephone call from Brian Ua Nualláin, a later Myles-na-gCopaleen!

"You're going to have a spot of bother tonight!"

It was the Maria Duce demonstration. But thank heavens for that small Dublin voice yelling from the gallery!

"Get out, ye dirty Protestants!"

Could have been another Fluther.

---

1. Mr. Harry Hutchinson died in Milan, 8th March, 1980.

O'CASEY AND THE TRADE UNIONS

JAMES PLUNKETT

In a letter from his home in London to Horace Reynolds dated February 6th, 1938, Seán O'Casey mentioned a recent visit from the labour leader, Jim Larkin and said, among other things:

"I had him with me the other evening with a friend, and we talked from early evening to the coming of the morn."

As, indeed, they would have. Both O'Casey and the veteran trade union leader were nearing their sixties, both were unstoppable talkers with a weakness for reminiscence, and both had shared together in the traumatic social and political upheavals which give the first two decades or so of Irish life in the twentieth century their strange mixture of pride and poverty, hunger, heroism and poltroonery and an elusive and scattered kind of grandeur. They had plenty to talk about. They would have talked of their mutual involvement in strikes and lock-outs, of rallies and gun-running, of foodships and soup kitchens and massive confrontations with law and religion. And, of course, of the personalities who had dominated the public imagination of the period. Many years later O'Casey, writing of these days, admitted that four buildings of the Dublin of those times remained, as he put it, forever in his heart and mind. They were his home, the church of St. Barnabas, the Abbey Theatre and Liberty Hall.

Liberty Hall had been the centre of the working class revolt against degrading conditions and, in considerable measure, of revolutionary nationalism, two movements which, as both men prophesied, were to prove incompatible.

After his father's death in middle life, O'Casey, who was six years old at the time, came to know the worst horrors of Dublin's tenement life and the extremes of its hunger and poverty. He was the last born of 13 children, eight of whom had died, a normal enough ratio in a city where the infant mortality rate was higher than Calcutta, then a plague spot. He was a sickly child, with a disease of the eyes, contracted from his unhygienic surroundings, which kept him from regular schooling and plagued him all his life. "Poverty, pain and penance," he was to write later, "those were the gates of Dublin — its three castles."

Religion pervaded his childhood, the more so perhaps because he was a Protestant child sharing to the full the deprivation of his predominantly Catholic neighbours. So, too, did the theme of war. As a young boy he saw his brothers and their friends going off in their colourful uniforms to fight the little, far-flung wars of Empire, and the songs of the household were those of the loyal soldiers of the Queen: "Over the burning sands of Egypt", for instance, or "Goodbye, Dolly, I must leave you". Yet, in spite of extreme poverty and a traditional attachment to the Crown, his first adult enthusiasm was neither for trade unionism nor Union Jacks but, surprisingly, for the ideals, even the excesses, of the Gaelic Revival. He adopted with enthusiasm the Celtic symbols of the harp and the round tower; he read with excitement about High Kings and kings not so high; he learned to speak Irish as best he could and fell in love with traditional Irish music. He even learned to play the bagpipes in a sort of a way and became founder and secretary of the St. Laurence O'Toole Pipers' Band. As a member of the Gaelic League he gaelicised his name to Seán Ó Cáthasaigh. He then joined the Irish Republican Brotherhood and took a hand in the militaristic euphoria of the times by trying his skill at patriotic verse. It was as outrageously banal as the general run of such work:

Beneath thy flag fresh hopes we feel
Ireland, dear Ireland
We'll gild its fold with glint of steel
And rifles' flame, dear Ireland.
In garish day, in night's damp dew
Its green and white and orange hue
Shall signal death to England's crew
And hope to thee, dear Ireland.

O'Casey could laugh at that later and write about it in self derision: "He glanced at the little, smoky lamp and fancied that it had changed to a candle — a tall, white, holy candle, its flame taking the shape of a sword; and, in its flaming point, the lovely face of Cathleen, the daughter of Houlihan."

Though he meant every word of it at the time, his everyday experience of the Gaelic League began to erode his faith in it, particularly its failure to stand up to the influence and pressures of the Catholic clergy. He saw its Portarlington Branch collapse when the local clergy objected because it was teaching Irish to mixed classes. Crossroad dances also met with disapproval and were abandoned. There were attacks on publications such as Ryan's *The Irish Peasant*. And he was bitterly upset at their failure to stand up for Dr. O'Hickey of Maynooth when he was dismissed for supporting the movement to have Irish as an essential subject in the new University.

As for the I.R.B. and their patriotic songs and stances — these, he decided, were mainly impractical daydreams — all guns and drums, as he was to put it, and no wounds. They were lost and dreaming in the romantic ecstacy of Thomas Davis's:

O for a steed, a rushing steed, on the Curragh
of Kildare
And Irish squadrons skilled to do what they are
ready to dare
A hundred yards, and England's guards
Drawn up to engage me there.

That was a bit too fustian for the realist in O'Casey. Besides, the Republican movement attracted the middle and lower middle classes in the main, not the general labourer. Few of them were of his kinship. His genuine brethren, he decided, were in the tottering houses among the poverty and the decay.

Needless to say, no man sheds one set of ideals totally on one day and replaces them with an entirely new set the next. There is overlapping, there is blending, there is a period when the new ideals are the unconscious motivation to action while the old ones seem still to rule the will and the mind. And so it seems to have been with O'Casey, until two events occurred which rooted out the old ideas finally and gave ascendancy to the new. The first of these was his discovery of the plays and prefaces of Bernard Shaw. The second and more immediate to the Dublin situation was the advent of Jim Larkin and the consequent massive eruption of trade union feeling. O'Casey set out the situation in a letter which will be found in the first volume of David Krause's work *The Letters of Seán O'Casey 1910-1941*. It is addressed to Horace Reynolds and is worth quoting at some length. It is the letter quoted earlier in which there is the reference to Larkin's visit. It is dated February 6th, 1938.

O'Casey writes:

"I had been for a good number o' years a member of the Irish Republican Brotherhood and an ardent nationalist. Then came the preaching of Jim Larkin and the books of Bernard Shaw. (By the way, it was a young Dublin nationalist named Kevin O'Loughlin, member of the third order of St. Francis, who introduced me to Shaw, by persuading me to read the sixpenny edition of *John Bull's Other Island*). These two great men swung me over to the left and I became critical of pure nationalism. But, still more was I critical of the workings of the I.R.B. It was making no progress, and appealed only to clerks and artisans — the great body of workers were set aside. Hardly a man of them knew how to use a hack or shovel, and nothing about the building of defences. But particularly I hated Bulmer Hobson, who was the white haired boy of Tom Clarke. Once Tom put me out of his shop because I criticised Hobson as Leader, and as Editor of *Irish Freedom:* Tom telling me he loved Bulmer as his own son.

"The I.R.B. took every help they could get (and they got a lot) from Jim Larkin's Union, and I did most of the work, for Jim was very fond of me. However, at a general meeting of the I.R.B. in Dublin I criticised its working. I was howled at by a lot, and supported by some; Bulmer, on the platform, drew a gun and there was pandemonium. So afterwards, with some others, I left the I.R.B. and flung myself into the Labour Movement, though still doing all I could for the National movement and P. H. Pearse's school St. Enda's and the St. Laurence O'Toole's Hurling and Football Club and Pipers' Band, which I founded and brought to a fine band with the help of chums."

The Larkin influence on O'Casey was the more immediate. Jim Larkin had come to Dublin in 1908 to organise the unskilled and casual workers of the city, the dockers, the carters and the factory workers. These were working long hours for starvation wages and lived for the most part in the appalling conditions of the tenement ghettoes of the city. Larkin, whose energy and oratory were unique, soon had them banding together to challenge the employers in strike after strike; and O'Casey, who had been working since

1903 as a general labourer with the Great Northern Railway of Ireland, joined Larkin's union in 1911. In December of that year he was dismissed from his job — no reason being given officially. The story is that he had been overheard attacking conditions in the railway and praising Jim Larkin's aggressive methods. He wrote a number of letters to the company requesting the reason for his dismissal and when the company declined to give reasons he published the correspondence in Larkin's paper, the *Irish Worker*. He was soon contributing regularly to its columns. Krause points to his letter urging workers to attend St. Enda's to see a pageant produced by Pearse, as one of many of his efforts to unite Labour and Nationalism. The letter is dated 7th June, 1913. In August of that year the epic chain of events began that quenched any lingering desire of his to reconcile the two.

A tram strike called by Larkin developed into a wholesale lockout which dragged on for over six months and involved about a third of the city. O'Casey, already unemployed, flung himself into the struggle. He worked in the food kitchens which were set up in the basement of Liberty Hall; he became secretary of the Women and Children's Relief Fund and later secretary of the Irish Citizen Army. He travelled the streets of Dublin in a borrowed horse and cart collecting funds and wrote several appeals for the pages of the *Irish Worker*.

As the lock-out dragged on and the poor suffered and starved, O'Casey's disillusionment with Nationalism and, in particular, with the Irish Volunteers, became total. In January 1914 he wrote an open letter to workers in the Volunteers which began with a quote from John Mitchell: "In a word, we demand Ireland for the Irish, not for the gentry alone".

It was a sentiment which became basic to the thinking of both Larkin and O'Casey.

"Workers," O'Casey wrote, "do you not think it is

high time to awake from your sleep and yield allegiance to no movement that does not avow the ultimate destiny of the workers."

In response to the Volunteers' declared determination "to secure and maintain the liberties and rights common to all Irishmen," O'Casey answered cynically: "We know the liberties and rights we enjoy: the right to toil till the blood is dried in our veins; the right to bless the land that gives us what it thinks we are worth; the right to suffer starvation, and misery, and disease, and then thank God that such light afflictions work an exceeding weight of glory. Workers, ye are fools to train and drill for anything less than complete enfranchisement, for the utter alteration of the present social system . . ."

His bitterness led to a clash with Countess Markiewicz, who was involved in both the Volunteers and the Citizen Army. O'Casey's case was that among the leadership of the Volunteers were employers who had locked out union members during the 1913 lockout and he tabled a motion at a meeting of the Citizen Army Council calling on her to sever her connection either with the Volunteers or the Citizen Army. His motion was defeated by one vote and O'Casey, in spite of Larkin's plea to the contrary, resigned as secretary, although he continued to write for the Army in the *Irish Worker*. Later, when he came to set out his thinking in a booklet called *The Story of the Irish Citizen Army*, published by Maunsell & Co. in 1918, he was more than ever convinced of the incompatibility of the Volunteer mentality and the aspirations of the trade union movement. He was also very conscious of the popular swing to the nationalistic stance of Sinn Féin, which the 1916 Rising and the executions of the leaders had brought about even among the general labourers and the casual workers:

"The activities of Sinn Féin are spreading over the land," he wrote, "and Labour comes halting very much behind."

He charged that Irish Labour propaganda was written from an English point of view and that its leaders were — as he put it — "painfully ignorant of their country's history, language and literature". Persecution had deepened the people's sympathy with their Irish origin and Irish Labour leaders would have to take the change into account if they were to win over the working class. Ultimately, he concluded, Labour would have to fight Sinn Féin. In the event, Labour backed off. O'Casey could do little about it and Larkin, who might have, was locked up in Sing Sing prison for subversive activities. By the time of his release and return to Ireland in 1923, the civil war had so politicised public thinking that social change was relegated to the back seats, where it remained for a generation.

Meanwhile, the Irish Transport & General Workers' Union, in the absence of Larkin in the United States from 1914 and his subsequent imprisonment there, had been built up and reorganised. One of the factors in its success was its involvement in the preparations for the insurrection of 1916, and its association with James Connolly who had become one of the executed leaders. On the new executive were men who considered Larkin too rash and too self-willed to be given the free hand with decisions he had had in the past, men who were not at all enthusiastic about the idea of his return to Ireland. The leader of this school of thought was William O'Brien, general treasurer of the union in 1919. O'Casey was now honorary secretary of the Jim Larkin Correspondence Committee, which was set up to organise a massive Christmas greeting from Irish workers to Larkin in Sing Sing. In 1921 William O'Brien ignored O'Casey's request for an interview about the greeting and, presumably, declined to sign the greeting himself. O'Casey also describes in *Inishfallen Fare Thee Well*, how he attempted to get the Dáil to call collectively for Larkin's release, but the

Treaty debate was at its height and unleashing hatreds which excluded everything other than themselves. The terrible beauty, O'Casey remarked, was beginning to lose her good looks. Cathleen Ní Houlihan had become oul snarley gob.

Trade Unionism was soon to follow the nationalists' bad example. When Larkin returned to Ireland in 1923 a quarrel broke out between himself and the Executive Committee, which resulted eventually in a Court case and his expulsion from the union he had founded. His followers then set up a breakaway union "The Workers' Union of Ireland". Who was to blame for the course of events is not of much importance today though Larkin himself must bear his share. What is worth remarking is that the seeds of the quarrel existed as far back as 1911. Correspondence between James Connolly and William O'Brien, published later on in O'Brien's book "The Attempt to Smash the Irish Transport & General Workers' Union" shows O'Brien encouraging Connolly's resentment of Larkin's almost total control of affairs. At the Trade Union Congress of 1914, under Larkin's presidency, there were muted clashes between the two of them, a rift which time failed to heal.

In O'Casey's eyes, the victory of the O'Brien faction over Larkin represented the triumph of compromise in the class struggle over a leader who saw trade unionism as a militant and revolutionary movement which would change the world. The impact on O'Casey of Larkin's first appearance on the Dublin scene is described in the autobiographies:

"Here was a man who would put a flower in a vase on a table as well as a loaf on a plate. Here, Seán thought, is the beginning of a broad and busy day."

Larkin's vision of trade unionism was one of a working class with access, not only to the necessities of food and work and shelter, but to all the graces of living: to music and poetry and pictures, to the countryside and the seaside, to education and intellectual pursuits. It excited O'Casey so much that he adopted it as his own. Nobody else but Larkin, he felt, could achieve it for the poor of Ireland, certainly, in O'Casey's eyes, not the O'Briens of this world. The thought was still with him when he paid tribute to Larkin on the Labour leader's death in 1947. "He was the first man in Ireland," O'Casey wrote in *The Irish Times*, "who brought poetry into the workers' fight for a better life." And it was with him, or so he asserts, when he was packing up to leave Ireland in disgust in 1926. He writes in *Inishfallen Fare Thee Well* — and the sense of loss is still there — "Seán packed his last few personal things into his one suitcase, the suitcase that had gone with him to Coole and was now to shepherd the things that would allow him to strut respectably through the streets of London. There was nothing to keep him in Ireland: he had no part in Cosgrave's Party, or in de Valera's policy; nor had he any in the Labour movement bossed by William O'Brien."

It was his farewell, not only to Inishfallen, but to active membership of the union, although he would certainly continue to champion working class causes all his long life. The truth was that his true star had been rising in another point in the heavens. Even during the trade union internecine trouble on Larkin's return in 1923 he had the first production of *The Shadow of a Gunman* at the Abbey to fill his mind and fire his ambitions, and *Juno and the Paycock* was already taking shape in his imagination, so that his letters are more and more concerned with the business of playwriting and hardly at all with the themes of political and social change. These issues, together with mankind's right to happiness and merriment and total freedom of choice, were to be presented as themes for drama. The redistribution of emphasis can be seen in a letter he wrote to Lady Gregory in January of 1925, asking her permission on Jim Larkin's behalf to stage

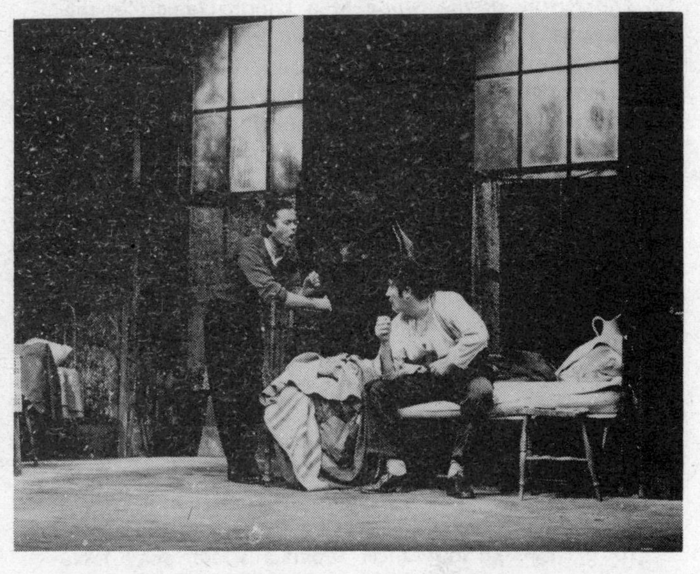

The Shadow of a Gunman
Desmond Cave as Donal Davoran and Donal McCann as Seamas Shields in the Abbey Theatre's 1980 production. (Photograph by Fergus Bourke.)

The Rising of the Moon at a Union concert in the Queen's. Permission was granted. Indeed, I remember young Jim Larkin giving an account of his father's performance in it. Big Jim Larkin held the view that there was no necessity to learn lines; he felt they would come naturally and spontaneously to him in the excitement of performance. The result, I understand, was hilarious, though it had little to do with Lady Gregory's play.

It was natural, of course, that O'Casey's experiences of trade unionism should get into his plays, just as did his political involvements and the events of his formative years in Dublin city. *The Star Turns Red* and *Red Roses For Me* are two specific examples, though *The Star Turns Red* is about the conflict between fascism and communism rather than the trade union struggle. It has Comrade Chief Red Jim in it, of course, and there is an all-out attempt by the police and the saffron shirts to break a strike, and an attempt to betray Jim by union officials which may have remote roots in the Dublin split of 1923; but it does not absorb and reflect back truly O'Casey's experience of the Dublin trade union upheavals on 1908-1914.

In *Red Roses For Me,* which, in addition, contains a fair amount of autobiography, the picture is closer to his real trade union experience and the dialogue and characterisation are more effective and evocative of the general membership which surrounded him in those Dublin days. Certainly, the aspirations expressed by the hero Ayamonn sound very much like those which flowered in O'Casey himself and which remained to inspire much of what he subsequently wrote.

And what, ultimately, did he get from his trade union experiences? First, perhaps, a wholesome rejection of a nationalistic will-o'-the-wisp which favoured revolution provided everyone in society continued to know his place. Second, a devotion to every "ism" of the Left which was so uncritical and unanalytical that it could become at times both tedious and shrill. Lastly and most importantly, however, trades unionism and nationalism and the Gaelic Revival were sources which supplied a gallery of characters behaving at their all-out worst or best. They surrounded him and reacted to him and he got the measure of them all: a bevy of narrow-minded, craw-thumping, mendacious and self-seeking middle-of-the-road men; a galaxy of under-privileged Joxers and Fluthers and Coveys and Brennans-of-the-Moor who were not entirely incapable of lapses into nobility, and who used a sort of boastful fantasy as a defence against the unremitting insults of a contemptuous and uncaring society; women of heroism and fortitude and instinctive compassion. And, in addition to all that, a personal view of human-kind which remained at bottom gay, ever hopeful and ever-aspiring. In the end, the gain surely repaid the suffering.

SEÁN O'CASEY AND SOCIALISM

C. DESMOND GREAVES

When Seán O'Casey died in 1964, he had behind him close on thirty years as an avowed communist, and twenty more as a labour sympathiser. There are, however, very few socialist characters in his plays, and with one exception, their functions tend to be secondary.

The first is Jimmie in the short political satire *Cathleen Listens In*. It was composed later than *The Shadow of a Gunman* but before *Juno and the Paycock,* and was first performed on October 1st, 1923. It reflects the mood of many Irish people at this time, one of bewilderment, disenchantment not without recrimination, and nostalgia for the "four glorious years". The civil war was over but its attitudes remained. O'Casey represents one section after another paying court to Cathleen, the new Ireland, Jimmie in the name of the neglected working class. He summarises the workers' position in the disillusioned words: "What's the good of loving Kathleen if she won't taken any notice of you?" He decides to take his affections elsewhere and declares "Socialism is the only hope of the workers".

There was no prospect of socialism at the time, as O'Casey well knew. The suggestion, therefore, seems to be, that the workers should opt out of the immediate struggles of the nation. This would be to do in the name of socialism precisely what Tom Johnson and William O'Brien appeared to be doing for reasons of prudence. There is, therefore, a strong possibility that O'Casey wished to satirise the Labour leaders.

In *Juno and the Paycock* the young man Jerry Devine whom Mary jilts in favour of the school teacher who has turned her head, is appointed a trade union organiser. When he learns that she has been thrown over, he approaches her again. "With Labour," he declares, "humanity is everything. We are leaders in the fight for a new life." But when he learns that she is pregnant he wonders that she can have fallen so low. His humanity, she muses, is just as narrow as the humanity of the others. This again is satire.

In *The Plough and the Stars* we have the Covey. Many of us have met him. He is the dogmatic self-proclaimed Marxian, who speaks in technicalities because, not really understanding the creed he professes, he cannot explain it in common or ordinary language.

There is no socialist in *The Silver Tassie* or *Within The Gates*. In *The Star Turns Red,* the hero, Jack, is a communist, and so is his girl friend. So, implicitly, is Red Jim, who obviously represents Larkin. The subject matter of this play is the forestalling of fascism by the seizure of power by the workers. It has been called propagandist, and that might be fair comment. But nobody who saw it when it was produced at the Abbey, could call it a weak play. Of all his plays, this was the nearest to O'Casey's convictions and it is one of his strongest.

Purple Dust contains no declared socialist, but *Oak Leaves and Lavender* has Drishogue, a communist. This play is more justly termed propagandist than any of the others. It concerns the British effort in the Second World War. Drishogue stands for the thousands of Irishmen who fought with distinction in the British forces, but as an Irishman and a communist, he insists that he is fighting not *for* England but *against* fascism. Perhaps this is why he is described as a thorn or a prickle.

The only other communist is Beoman in *Behind the*

Green Curtains. This is O'Casey's most pessimistic play, set in an imaginary provincial town dominated by religious dictators and their pious hangers-on. Freshness, vigour and nobility can only survive by escape. A factory manager refuses to dismiss the parties to a mixed marriage. Sectarian strong-arm men raid his house. Beoman, who is present, seizes one of their weapons and successfully defends himself. The others give in. As his name implies he symbolises the life-force. But it is a life-force on the defensive.

Leaving aside *The Star Turns Red*, there are only five clearly distinguishable socialists in the whole body of O'Casey work, and of these the three in his early plays are not sympathetically drawn. A publisher writes for a dust cover "O'Casey was a working class rebel who put socialism first" or again "His poverty-stricken upbringing in the Dublin slums led him to suspect the fanatical idealism of the nationalists". These pronouncements are based, not on the plays, but on the autobiography. O'Casey's political outlook informed his plays. But one cannot draw it mechanically out of them. For example, on the strength of *The Silver Tassie*, attempts have been made to represent O'Casey as a pacifist. But what of *The Star Turns Red*? There the workers take over the apparatus of state by force of arms. Obviously O'Casey's work cannot be summarised in a few simple phrases. He was concerned with the whole of life, and more particularly with the cultural, spiritual and intellectual life of the Irish people, within which the tradition of socialism is one historical strand. There is a universality in the plays which is absent from the life story.

It is a well-known principle that it is dangerous to judge people from their consciousness of themselves. And indeed if O'Casey's account of his political development is emotionally true, historically it is frequently inaccurate. In 1963 he wrote "I abandoned the romantic cult of nationalism sixty years ago". That would be in 1903. But that was the year in which he joined the Gaelic League. In 1905 he brought Ernest Blythe into the Irish Republican Brotherhood, and he himself remained a member until at least 1913. In that year, in the course of a controversy in the I.R.B. periodical *Irish Freedom*, he strongly resisted the suggestion that, after gaining her independence, Ireland should be reconstructed upon a socialist model.

He was a man for involved sentences and I will have to do the best I can with this quotation. "Woe unto us," he wrote, "if we hand over our ideals to be squared and shaped and glossed by those who would write in our skies that socialism is Ireland's hope, and hang round our necks the green ribbons of Cumannacht na hÉireann." Cumannacht na hÉireann was James Connolly's party, otherwise known as the Socialist Party of Ireland. He was criticising it from a nationalistic position. In another controversy proceeding at the same time, he deliberately excluded Connolly, because Connolly stood for the primacy of national independence. O'Casey's nationalist commitment ceased to be absolute after 1913, but he was writing election ballads for Sinn Féin as late as 1918.

It would, of course, be quite wrong to accuse O'Casey of deception. I met him only once. Nobody who spent five minutes in his company could fail to recognise a rock of integrity. He was a man who lived with and in his imagination. He *felt* as if he had been a socialist for sixty years. And those who wrote about him in his lifetime were quite right not to question his feelings about himself.

But thanks to the researches of Professor Margulies, Mr. Anthony Butler and others, we now know something of O'Casey's early life and development. He was not born in the slums. He was born into a cultured middle-class family. His father described himself on one occasion as a law clerk, on another as an accountant. With the exception of Seán himself, all the children attended the Central Model Schools at which a small fee was paid. His father could read Latin. His sister Isabella learned to play the piano. In the eighteen-eighties the possession of a piano was a fair test of middle-class respectability. These were no tenement dwellers. The houses where they lived are still standing today and are still not slums, even after nearly a century.

At the same time O'Casey had experiences which undoubtedly prepared his mind for the socialism he later espoused. When he was six years old his father died. Three years later his brothers Michael and Thomas enlisted. Then Isabella married. O'Casey and his mother were for a period dependent on Isaac's fifteen shillings a week. This was far from a princely salary, but let us bear in mind the fact that many a regularly employed carter or general labourer had to maintain six children on less. O'Casey's family unquestionably took a tumble in the world. But they did not hit rock bottom, and after 1894 prosperity returned and was sustained for twenty years.

Like many gifted young people, O'Casey was an enthusiast. His first enthusiasm was religion. He spoke eloquently at prayer meetings. He supported foreign missions. He taught in the Sunday School. He pored over the Bible until he knew chapters by heart. He remained absorbed in the affairs of the parish of St. Barnabas until 1905, when he had differences with the Minister, the Reverend Morgan Griffin. These differences arose from the second of his altruistic enthusiasms, the Irish-Ireland movement. He was active in the promotion of the Irish language within the Protestant community. At some point he encountered what Patrick Pearse called the "murder machine". He wrote an attack on the system of national education, which he believed was destroying the basis of Irish culture. He showed it to the Minister, who told him that he ought to be in jail.

This was his transition to politics, but not to socialist politics, even though he was now working as a labourer on the Great Northern Railway. It is of course a fallacy that a man is made a socialist by doing hard work for poor pay, or by living in a slum. If he has lived in a nice house and is then forced into a slum, he may feel rebellious. But if he is born and bred there he may think it the most natural place on earth. It was when O'Casey was victimised after taking part in the 1911 rail strike that he began to interest himself in Labour politics. He became a staunch trade unionist and fell under the influence of Larkin.

Larkin was probably the strongest political influence in O'Casey's life. He idolised him. When Larkin's name was mentioned to O'Casey as an old man, his eyes would light up. O'Casey was locked out for refusing to sign the document promising not to remain or become a member of the Irish Transport and General Workers' Union. He was extremely active in the period of the lock-out, being responsible for raising relief. After 1913 he was a Labour man. But he did not describe himself as a socialist. In political matters he reacted as a nationalist. In economic matters he was a trade unionist. From the interplay of these two principles, perhaps we can explain much that seems a trifle erratic in his behaviour over the next few years.

It was Desmond Ryan who remarked that O'Casey's mind could hold only one enthusiasm at a time. He broke with the I.R.B. because it would not commit its military force to the defence of the locked out workers. He was bitterly opposed to the Volunteers because, since their leaders included employers, he thought they must be antagonistic to the working class at every point. He broke with the Citizen Army because it permitted Countess Markiewicz to continue her association with Cumann na mBan, which O'Casey considered a middle-class organisation.

Thanks to his break with the Citizen Army, he took no part in the Rising of 1916, though there is evidence that he afterwards regretted this. In later life he claimed to have argued against a proposed insurrection. But his first published comment upon it, in a pamphlet designed to commemorate Thomas Ashe, glorifies it, and with rare sunburstry. At this time he was constantly predicting the outbreak of political hostilities between Labour and Sinn Féin. This perspective was foreshadowed at the August 1917 meeting of the Irish Trade Union Congress, and must have been common currency in Labour circles.

But when did O'Casey become a socialist in the strict sense of the word? I am aware of no surviving document from this period in which he clearly so describes himself. At this time socialism in Ireland meant Connolly. In a letter published in Dr. Krause's collection, dated March 16th, 1918, O'Casey writes about a meeting of the "Irish Socialist Party", getting its name wrong, but does not say he attended. On April 9th he quotes Connolly as an authority. Six years later, speaking to Lady Gregory about events supposed to have happened around this time, he said "I was a socialist then". But R. J. Connolly does not remember his taking part in the activities of the Socialist Party of Ireland. And to make matters even more difficult to understand, on December 3rd, 1919, George Bernard Shaw wrote to him, in reference to a pamphlet which had been submitted for his opinion, saying "Why do you not come out definitely on the side of Labour and the English language?" I am inclined to think that he first became interested in socialism in 1918, but that while always a staunch "Labour man", he was not strongly committed. His centring of his political activities round various committees concerned with the return to Ireland of Larkin would tend to confirm this opinion. His remark to Lady Gregory, implying that he was no longer a socialist, explains his satirical treatment of the characters Jimmy, Jerry Devine and the Covey.

Early in 1919 he revised his opinion of the Rising. His *The Story of the Irish Citizen Army* is an attack on Connolly's policy of an alliance with the Republicans in an effort to win national independence. From his denial of Connolly's right to be described as a "socialist martyr" one would gather that O'Casey was a socialist himself. But he does not say so. He cannot have understood Connolly's purpose, which was set out in world-famous words:

> "Starting thus, Ireland may yet set the torch to an European conflagration that will not burn out until the last throne and the last capitalist bond and debenture will be shrivelled on the funeral pyre of the last war lord".

O'Casey implies that Connolly had abandoned internationalism, though there is no doubt about the internationalism of the statement I have quoted. Indeed the position of classical Irish socialism was that internationalism was only possible on a national basis. Irish socialism was derived, by way of Chartism, from the programme of reform published by the United Irishmen in 1792. Daniel O'Connell gave it to the Chartists, together with their name. Feargus O'Connor added the plank of the repeal of the Union. It was then possible to establish Chartist clubs in Ireland. The lesson is clear. It is only possible for English and Irish workers to have a common programme if the essence of that programme as far as Ireland is concerned is *separation*.

This was the position of the International Working Men's Association, whose Dublin section was founded by McEvatt, the Fenian and veteran of 1848. His daughter was married to J. P. McDonnell, who represented Ireland on the General Council. An attack on

McDonnell's policy of establishing Irish sections in Britain received a reply from Frederick Engels which summarises the classical position:

> "In a case like that of the Irish, true internationalism must necessarily be based on a distinct national organisation, and they were under the necessity to state in the preamble to their rules that their first and most pressing duty as Irishmen was to establish their own national independence."

In 1872, under the attacks of the followers of Bakunin and Lassalle, the International began to break up. A variety of dogmatisms affected Dublin socialism, among them the notion that internationalism could be disembodied from its national basis and it was Connolly's achievement to make the classical position once more accepted by the majority. He did not, however, achieve unanimity, and after his death there was no theoretician of comparable status to continue the tradition. It is of great importance to appreciate that all the evidence points to the fact that O'Casey became a socialist after Connolly's death. The ante-dating of his political involvement has made it all but incomprehensible.

The years 1918 to 1922 were years of limitless hope both for the Labour and national movements. When the edifice came crashing down O'Casey felt disoriented, and this doubtless played a part in his decision to go to England. He arrived in London in March 1926, and apart from voting Labour in the election of 1929, seems to have left politics alone. During this period of political inactivity he dedicated himself to his art, in which he tried to serve what Toller called "the eternal powers of life, truth, joy, beauty, freedom, the mind and the spirit".

But in 1933, in one of the classical centres of

The Star Turns Red
Edward Golden as Red Jim and Patrick Laffan as The Purple Priest in Tomás Mac Anna's first Irish production, 1978.

civilisation, a regime established itself which was determined to blot these things out. The invasion of Abyssinia by Hitler's Italian ally, showed that the new barbarism was expansionist. There was nothing for it but to abandon artistic seclusion and join the hurly-burly of politics. O'Casey did this unhesitatingly, in company with all that was best in the intellectual life of Europe.

There can be little doubt that his transition from the somewhat vague communism which he shared with Bernard Shaw, to the Marxism he proclaimed in 1937, was the product of his opposition to fascism. In this both the western communists and the U.S.S.R. were playing an important part. This was the background to *The Star Turns Red*. A fascist plot is foiled by a communist take-over. The nominal setting of the play is Dublin. But it presents a European dilemma. In it O'Casey celebrates his decision to support communism.

For over twenty-five years he identified himself with the broad perspectives of the British Communist Party, though he never became a member. His identification with the U.S.S.R. was even closer, and on one occasion he composed a prose poem to that country which is so extravagantly enthusiastic that it is embarrassing to read. This did not, however, deter him from sending protests when Zhdanof tried to prescribe by order the forms of artistic composition.

Immediately before and during the early part of the war, he took up the issue of the partition of Ireland, not, however, from the position of the Irish classical socialist, but from the internationalist standpoint of the British socialist. He followed Irish events closely and did not hestitate to comment. He was very scornful when the Irish Labour Party accepted seats in the first Inter-party Government. Throughout the last twenty years of his life his cheque book was always available for any socialist group which might spring up in

Ireland. He was convinced that the country was groaning under a clerical yoke, and that only socialism could liberate it.

I have said there are few socialist characters in O'Casey's plays. There are, however, many characters which imply socialism by challenging commercial values. Indeed, once O'Casey had completed his first stage of development with *The Silver Tassie* he provided each play with at least one of them. One can instance The Dreamer in *Within the Gaters,* O'Killigain in *Purple Dust,* Ayamonn in that fine play *Red Roses For Me,* and above all Loreleen in the satirical extravaganza *Cock-a-Doodle-Dandy*. Here every commercial value is stood on its head and ridiculed. O'Casey says in effect, "isn't it better sense to enjoy a dance and a drink than to pile up figures in a ledger?"

These anti-commercial characters are the clue to how O'Casey understood socialism. It was not a dogma or an abstraction. He sought from it what he had once sought in the Christian religion, in the non-commercial values of Ireland's past, in the pursuit of his art. His devotion to this bordered on the quixotic. He made a little money; but he never altered a principle for the sake of it. He never concealed his opinions. Head-strong always, at times some will think wrong-headed, he held before him a vision of a world where people would behave as human beings rather than as animated calculating machines. It is said that anger makes the poet. It was out of his anger against all that stunts and debases human life that O'Casey constructed the greatest plays of the twentieth century.

O'CASEY STAGE PRODUCTIONS IN THE GERMAN DEMOCRATIC REPUBLIC

HANS-GEORG SIMMGEN
(translated by Sigrid and Richard Weber)

For twelve years on the stage of the Berlin Theatre at the Schiffbauerdamm, traditional headquarters of the "Berliner Ensemble", founded by Bertholt Brecht and Helene Weigel, the deliberately shabby, heavy velvet curtain rose to the music of an Irish melody rendered in the style of an heroic overture, the occasion being the performance of *Purple Dust* by Seán O'Casey. The production which had its first performance in 1966 has since been repeated a few hundred times,* and has become a legend within the consciousness of this country as well as abroad.

Again and again during the overture the large artificial spider crept tirelessly out of the folds of the carefully prepared curtain and the two contrived rats made their gala appearance in front of the curtain by emerging from the holes in the prompter's box. Finally, one got to view the interior and the magic world of the old Tudor-style castle hall. Here the Irish craftsmen moved into action, emerging from holes beneath the floors as well as from the holes in the free-hanging Irish coffered

*Translator's note: The Brecht-Theatre is a repertory theatre. Therefore *Purple Dust* was not played "en suite" but only once or twice per week, alternating with the other productions in the repertory. Thus the "few hundred times" over a span of 12 years. Each performance was, however, a special occasion as the translator can testify, having seen the opening performance as well as another later on in 1966/67.

ceiling. Here hens cackled and a theatrical cow went for a stroll, munching grass. Here a huge grass-roller breaks through a castle wall; there a table gets jammed within a too small doorway; until finally all dissolves into dust, into *Purple Dust,* and becomes a huge basin of water in which are cheerful Irish fish bursting with life.

During this time, many thousands of spectators heard the message of the great Irish writer and rebel many hundreds of times. They were fascinated by the great poetic wealth and vitality of his work which filled their hearts and minds with new joie de vivre. This tremendous gift of strength for a new joy in living was the governing factor of this production, and it was the magnet which drew the spectators to O'Casey as if to a richly-laid table full of delicacies.

In previous years Brecht and his disciples had already shown a preference for writers from the island of Ireland when making up the comedy repertory for their theatre. In 1955 a Brecht-adaptation of Farquhar's *Recruiting Officer* was staged under the title *Trumpets and Drums* in Berlin (the Berliner Ensemble under Helene Weigel gave a guest performance in London of this production in 1956). This was followed in 1956 by John Millington Synge's *Playboy of the Western World* (translated by Anna E. Wiede and Peter Hacks, and with music by Hanns Eisler). Then a few years later, circa 1963, a group of young colleagues became fascinated by the attractive but difficult text of *Purple Dust*. From the beginning, a young playwright (Helmut Baierl) and a young set-designer (Andreas Reinhardt) together with the director, were members of this group. This system of mobilising stage productions as team work was a characteristic trait of the Brecht Theatre, as well as of Brecht's collective way of working, throughout which all the elements of the theatre, including those pertaining to the practical realisation of the production, were acting simultaneously, rather than consecutively, to achieve the desired goal. Given this complex way of progressing, the task of the German-text translation was a very big problem indeed. At that time there was no satisfactory way of rendering the peculiar and unique quality of O'Casey's diction in German. Most often O'Casey was translated without heeding his truly gigantic theatrical vision. The translations were glib, exact and philological. The interrelations between the characters, which are also discernible within their speech, were not considered; their specific theatrical situation was not fully expressed. What we tried to do was to achieve new and more conclusive scripts, without losing the irregularities and without ignoring the social and dialect-bound peculiarities in which O'Casey's texts so richly abound. O'Casey's abundance itself was what interested us, not the mere information of the existence of such abundance. Under the tutelage of such masters of our theatre as Manfred Wekwerth, Karl von Appen and Elisabeth Hauptmann (a long-time collaborator of Brecht) there came into being something like an artistic German/non-German O'Casey-diction, a brittle almost synthetic dialect, which had been stylised after having been drawn from everyday gesture, and which had its own syntax and certain known or hitherto unknown dialect colourings. Poetic and lyrical passages were deliberately made to stand out. Such a text was able to support and motivate the actions of the characters. It was able to carry, as well as provoke, the individual peculiarities of each character. In particular, the social-critical passages could now be poetically rendered — and precisely this poetic form of social criticism appeared to us as the best and purest O'Casey. Such a basic and picturesque language, far removed from glib conversational dialogue, gave a firm framework to the robust stage fun in *Purple Dust,* and kept it from losing itself in the absurd or a merely fun-for-fun's sake

Purple Dust
John Kavanagh as Basil Stoke, Edward Golden as Barney, billie Morton as Cloyne and the late Pitt Wilkinson as Cyril Poges in the first Abbey production, 1975. (Photograph by Fergus Bourke.)

theatre clowning. By this laborious but rewarding work we gained access to the play, in which O'Casey in his amusing manner describes throughout three acts nothing else but the bankruptcy (spiritual as well as material) of an historically framed idyll, in which the real heroes are the ordinary people, the building workers of Irish origin, who are called upon to preserve the idyll. However, before one can destroy anything in the theatre, even if it is only an old derelict Tudor castle, one has to erect it lovingly, unashamedly, with as much imagination as possible. Both worlds, which collide here, could thus be shown lovingly, as well as seductively, according to their own value or non-value as a challenge to the spectators to sharpen their own imagination and to make their own judgement.

Co-translator Helmut Baierl formulated his own opinion at the time in approximately this way: "O'Casey is a damn tricky person. What appears with him to be insignificant is always of the greatest significance. Contrary to Ibsen. For O'Casey's characters, mere speaking assumes the quality of action. It is significant not merely what somebody says, but how and at what length something is being said. The Irish bricklayers get on the nerves of the Englishmen with their speaking alone."

Brecht taught us to consider the "story" of a play as the starting point for a production. But even the search for the so-called "story" in this play was not an easy one. In O'Casey the stories are hidden away at a great depth. Every sentence is filled to the brim with reality — but in order to render such sentences in a way that can be fully understood, the whole play has to be transported into its own particular world — and thus also every single sentence. Only then does the sentence gain the brilliance of O'Casey's own special manner, which one has to call "realistic".

At this point the next step had to be taken by the set

designer who had to discover for himself this play's very particular world. The stage design had to lend reality to the world of the play — as opposed to everyday reality. The degree to which reality would be changed or violated in this would be governed by the degree of heightening in the spoken text itself as much as by its own characteristic traits. The stage design could not be naturalistic in an illustrative way, but had to be drawn from the specific textual realism, in order to give resonance to O'Casey's poetic quality.

Armed with these ideas and intentions we endeavoured in 1964 to stage *Purple Dust* in Gera, a town in Thuringia, as a kind of trial run for Berlin. For the opening night in March, this being the World Theatre Day, we had invited Seán O'Casey to attend. Because of his great age he was, however, unable to travel anymore. But he sent us a telegram: ". . . send greetings now all warm wishes to you and your group for success of Purple Dust — O'Casey." His good wishes came true that evening. And I remember clearly how delighted we were with his greetings, and how hard we were hit by the news of his death later that same year.

We were left with the task of responding to O'Casey's strong theatrical and textual visions with further practical attempts at staging. It was a very special evening when finally, in February 1966, *Purple Dust* opened in the theatre of the Berliner Ensemble. The critic Günther Cwoydrak wrote the following about it in the weekly *The World Stage:* "The BE performed *Purple Dust,* as it were, like a posthumous meeting between O'Casey and Brecht. Both have a lot in common: they were social realists as well as real socialists; both left behind a lifetime's work, full of intellectual energy and lyric beauty, which places them at the top of the dramatic world literature of our century. But — one should not overlook the differences, and I am only speaking now of their dramatic works: Brecht's poetic lines of argument are concentrated, brief; the pleasure is logical in the manner in which logic gives pleasure. O'Casey's plays by contrast are not less consistent, but are less concentrated; they do not delve any less deeply, but they do spread out more; they are basically rational, but romantic in many a detail and episode; sometimes they are lyrically abandoned and the final result is drawn less summarily."

"Here in this production O'Casey and Brecht met — and it turned out to be a meeting worth viewing. O'Casey was divided by Brecht — and O'Casey was multiplied. Every detail, every sentence was taken to task with regard to its necessity, its function; the realism of the play was dipped in a bright, sharp, and sometimes garish light. No corner remained in the dark. The satirical contours stood out harshly and precisely. Such a performance of O'Casey, where a play is both divided as well as multiplied, would of course be only conceivable in the Berliner Ensemble; and the calculation left over no remainder: knowledge and pleasure made their twin appearance."

At this point it may be in order to say a few words about this "Berliner Theater". Since its foundation in 1949 it had a special status, with Bertholt Brecht (as its chief adviser and producer) supervising the work of all colleagues. Even after his death in 1956, his disciples under the guidance of Helene Weigel tried to continue his work. In the 1960s, even, Brecht's plays were staged according to his ideas: *The Threepenny Opera, The Resistible Rise of Arturo Ui, The Days of the Commune* as well as Shakespeare's *Coriolanus* and Wischnewski's *Optimistic Tragedy*.

The danger of stylistic mannerism, which was theoretically conceivable, was never a fault of this theatre, since that would have been fundamentally inconsistent with Brecht's working method, the chief characteristic of which was "change": That is, philosophically speaking, Brecht was a man of dialectics, and applied this method also to his theatre. Nor did his pupils remain idly seated behind the solid wall of the so-called Brechtian theory, but packed the knowledge of their teacher into their rucksacks and travelled in order to explore new lands, metaphorically speaking. Some excursions brought little back home in the way the public had expected. But each metaphorical excursion to the Green Isle, to O'Casey's beloved island, which O'Casey viewed with one "laughing" and one "weeping" eye, led us to a fortunate homecoming.

The beauty of O'Casey's ideas in his play *Purple Dust*, which challenges the strength of the people, was received with enthusiasm by the Berlin audience. It was an audience which lived and worked with these ideas. It had written these ideas — as vital energy — on their banners. An immense contradiction of our times became clear: "Back to Nature — but let us remain in business in spite of that!" In O'Casey's comedy this theme is introduced as a major Stock Exchange manipulation. But this theme then collapses, faced with the reality of real life and concrete truth. The endeavour to heal the world through the power of money is confronted with the reality of social inequality. The play's finale with thunderstorm, thunder and lightning, makes for more sense and logic than the logic of the monied people.

During May of 1966 a memorable meeting took place in Berlin. Mrs. Eileen O'Casey travelled via Prague to Berlin to meet Helene Weigel in the Brecht Theatre, and saw a performance of *Purple Dust*. In the course of an interview with the *Berliner Zeitung* she said the following:

"*Purple Dust* — that was wonderful! Mrs. Weigel had warned me: the production was a little crazy. But: it's bound to be. For especially within the craziness lies the comic quality of the play. The good thing is that O'Casey's message does not go by the board." And she continued: "There are theatres, where people believe that plays with a critical social content have to be performed solemnly. But that was not Seán's intention. There is everywhere lurking a great deal of humour, and this humour was beautifully seen here. It makes me very happy to experience the way in which O'Casey is honoured and loved here."

It was comparatively late when people here began to occupy themselves with O'Casey's plays. Following a first performance of *The Shadow of a Gunman* in the "German Theatre" (Deutsches Theater) in Berlin in 1954, there were only about four further O'Casey productions within the next decade. The Berlin production suffered under the misapprehension that O'Casey had to be firmly placed among the writers who followed in the tradition of Naturalism. Thus, one was too much preoccupied with the exact rendering of the environment. The dialectic of comic versus tragic elements within the structure of the play, as well as within the characters, was not recognised. As a result, the story of the writer and rebel-against-his-will was interpreted too one-sidedly as tragic, and the overall effect was very schematic.

The staging of *Red Roses For Me* in 1963 in the same theatre was also predominantly governed by the conception of a "naturalistic" O'Casey. The poetic quality of the language was rendered in a too rational and dry style. The musical quality of the writing did not achieve the quality of song. Individual variety and psychological wealth were missing. No bridges were erected between an historically concrete portrayal and the poetic power of symbols.

Only since the middle 1960s can a new period of O'Casey acceptance be discerned. Only from this time onwards can one talk about a serious occupation with

O'Casey within the theatres of this country, which does justice to his work.

Aside from the already discussed productions in 1964 in Gera and in 1966 in Berlin by Helmut Baierl and Hans-Georg Simmgen, there was another much noted and effective O'Casey production of the one-act plays, *Hall of Healing, A Pound on Demand,* and *The Moon Shines on Kylenamoe* staged by Maik Hamburger and Adolf Dresen in the German Theatre in Berlin in 1965. It was these two different productions that provided an impetus, as well as set a standard, for the new O'Casey trend. Both productions, which in their artistic solutions and in the method they employ differ to a great extent from each other, did have essential and fundamental points in common. Both productions took their impulse from a creative and critical advancement of Brecht's theatre work, from a retrospective recollection of the basic elements of his theatre practice, which is founded on a realism rooted in the people. This theatrical practice, which encompasses a critical view of one's own theories and insights, not only fertilised Brecht's own works, but also the works of other epochs and cultures. This philosophical attitude, termed "critical attitude" by Brecht, opened new ways for practical theatre work and thus opened the paths and avenues towards O'Casey and his writings.

Both Berlin productions made their point through their fascination with a contradictory portrayal of the ordinary people in O'Casey's plays. This fascination showed itself especially in the way in which language is used as a mobiliser of action, story and characters, and was entirely novel to our theatre practice, providing as it did, new possibilities for defining the interrelations between the characters.

Manfred Wekwerth, who today is the manager and main director of the Berliner Ensemble, made the following comment with regard to this phenomenon:

"Language does not only make action possible in this play, but is already action on its own!" How somebody says something is of enormous importance. It is nearly more important than what he says.

Character conflicts are caused by the simple fact that a common language cannot be found. Leaving aside its function as a means of communication, language had also become a means of misunderstanding as demonstrated by the English lord in *The Moon Shines on Kylenamoe* whose relation with the common people breaks down because of language. Two persons confront each other face to face and honestly explain the facts to each other, and the other person says "yes" meaning precisely the opposite. This mode of portraying absurd relations and attitudes in life, may make one think a little distantly of Beckett's way of writing. However, with O'Casey everything is clearly motivated, whereas in Beckett it is often hard to penetrate. The portrayal of absurd relationships between people does not always have to result in absurd theatre.

In order to achieve productions with a high standard of intricate relationship between language and action, new translations were of the utmost importance. Philological exactness was no longer enough and neither was the glib routine of dialogues originating from the bourgeois salon drama. Thus it was not by chance that the new translations were created by people involved in theatrical practice, e.g. Maik Hamburger, Adolf Dresen and Hans-Georg Simmgen, who were all able to test out their new texts, prior to completion, during rehearsal. The original lyrical talent of the young GDR-writer Helmut Baierl was helpful, but often enough, some of the actors had a brilliant idea resulting from their sense of language and their involvement with O'Casey's plots.

Until 1975, ninety-five O'Casey productions could be counted in the German Democratic Republic and eighty-seven of these were staged after 1965. The unusual interest in O'Casey's plays since 1965 had other reasons than those that are to be found within the realm of theatre and theatre aesthetics. This can be traced to the realm of social interest and its changing demands. During the mid-sixties a new social situation arose in East Germany and became more defined as time went by. Historically, this can be explained by saying that the consciousness of the people was no longer preoccupied with the pros and cons of socialism. Now the individual gained a new interest. Having created these new conditions, it was of interest to him to see how he had created them. The individual more and more wanted to learn to understand himself, socially speaking, as his own creator. This not only changed the themes of the theatre but also its function.

Here O'Casey's stories, bursting with life and his rich portrayal of people, created a strong degree of interest. Featuring man as the creator of his own circumstances of life was a distinguishing feature of O'Casey's plays and made him a writer of and for our times, with much to tell us here and now. These facts and perhaps others as well, led to many interesting productions. To name but a few, there were: *The Star Turns Red* (1967) in Rostock as well as in Berlin (1969) at the Maxim Gorki Theatre; *Cock-a-Doodle-Dandy* (1969) in Leipzig, in Berlin (1971) and in Potsdam (1976); and *The Bishop's Bonfire* (1970) in Dresden and Potsdam and a television production; *Juno and the Paycock* (1972) in the Berlin German Theatre and in Zwickau; *Purple Dust* (1972) in Magdeburg; and *Red Roses For Me* in Karl Marx City.

Needless to say, there are still problems of interpretation which should not be overlooked, and which still make O'Casey's plays difficult. These have to do with the involvement of theatre practice in its totality, as well as with the fact that the individual Irish national sensibility is, naturally, strange to our public. What is often no more than a pointed portrayal of Irish national character, may appear to our public as remote, or even "exotic". Some productions may suffer from uncertainty of diction. Either the picturesque language has been reduced to plain naturalism or, at the other extreme, is often rendered as a kind of recitation on stage. Both extremes are wrong and violate the dramatic quality of the language that expresses itself through the quality of gesture. Great and exemplary performances were given by some of the best actors, for example, Martin Flörchinger, Hilmar Thate or Dieter Franke. As it happened, the best actors were just good enough for the interpretation of O'Casey's plays. The utmost demands were made on the art of acting and its technique.

Naturally enough, even today there are no ready-made recipes for the performance and playing of O'Casey, but, as I see it, the adventure of an O'Casey production starts with the actor, and not so much with the interpretation of the story. It is the actor who lends individual life to O'Casey's characters on the stage. If one may say, metaphorically speaking, that the way to O'Casey's Ireland was only made possible by the Brechtian bridge, there is no doubt whatsoever that, during the years that followed, the Irishman's mode of writing, and his conception of character, led to productive criticism of a formerly too didactic interpretation of Brecht.

In the future, too, O'Casey's plays will remain a measuring rod and provocation to keep all the means of theatrical expression in a state of lively movement. This goes to explain the great affection that theatre people feel for O'Casey, who not alone endeavoured to change the theatre, but also the world itself.

O'CASEY: THE POSE IN THE PROSE

ROBERT HOGAN

Lately some critical people have questioned the authenticity of Seán O'Casey's autobiographies, but even the well-disposed have always noted the absence of hard fact in those six remarkable books. Yet, in the only essential sense, these books are as hard, exact and authentic as it is possible for an autobiography to be. They catch, vividly and precisely and fully, the real, the rich character of the man; and that, surely, is the main thing that a life story must do. If a life story, whether biography or autobiography, fails in that, it fails in everything.

Think of those many, fat, leather-bound, top-edges-gilt, two-decker lives of Great Victorians — books stuffed with facts and dates and everything possible, except life. Last year I read Sir Alfred Lyall's biography of Lord Dufferin, and learned everything important, except why and what.

The great life story in the English language is, of course, Boswell's *Life of Johnson,* which was published in 1791. In the nearly 200 years since then, Boswell has been contradicted and corrected, amended and amplified, and really superseded in every possible way except intrinsic excellence. If you want to know Samuel Johnson as an — in every sense of the word — breath-taking man, you must not go to the knowledgable modern biographers; you must go to Boswell. Similarly, if you want to know the live, breath-taking O'Casey, you must go to O'Casey.

Yet how can that be said when there is hardly a date

mentioned in his entire six volumes? When, as some writers have argued with some plausibility, O'Casey ignored, suppressed, exaggerated and distorted? When central, even shattering facts of his life are not even touched upon? When his views of certain well-known public personages are so strange that those figures are nearly unrecognisable? When, for much of the later volumes, you get no exact or concrete sense of the ordinary, prosaic world about him? When, finally, his whole life story seems so camouflaged by, so enveloped and utterly swaddled in, that famous and flamboyant prose style?

But perhaps the answer lies just there — in his prose style. Buffon said that the style is the man. If an autobiography is honest and true, it reflects what the author saw that was to him important. An autobiography is made up of an arrangement of words, of a choice of words in certain chosen juxtapositions. It is made up of a style, and a true and honest style is a reflection of an author's outer eyes and also of his inner eyes. That is, of what he saw, and of what he thought and felt about what he saw. That is, of his world, and his brain, and his soul. The true style is the true man, and nowhere more revealingly than when the man wrote about himself.

When O'Casey was alive, what he was like was known, casually or intimately, and more or less truly, by the few hundred people who lived with him, or worked with him, or talked with him. If you asked any of those people what he was like, their answers might have comprised a number of things — what he did, what he said, what he looked like, the expressions on his mobile face, how his voice sounded, his gestures, his habits, what kind of food he liked to eat, what kind of pipe tobacco he liked to smoke, certainly how he dressed, and maybe even how he would peer at the television with his face almost touching it. Yet most of those details would have been finally so trivial. When he was an old man, he looked marvellous — bony, frail, tolerantly cocky, bemused, and with a costume much too flamboyant for his weakening body, although appropriate enough for his ever-strengthening spirit. Now that he is dead, he can be a bit recaptured by his moving shadow on a few feet of film and by the ghost of his voice on a few recordings. But to find more than a shadow or a ghost, you have to go to what he wrote, and perhaps for a writer that is always the best and truest place to go.

I would say, then, that the truth and even the falsity of the man O'Casey is most fully and clearly to be found in what he wrote about himself. In the prose of the autobiography, the style was, and the style is, the man; and whoever says O'Casey was lying in those six books knows nothing about autobiography or truth or style or men.

One could say that there are three kinds of prose writers: the individualist, the conformist and the zombie. All zombies write badly. Their minds have been programmed by the medium of the less than medium media, or by the literary protocol of the civil service, or by the jargon of methodologies that have to be methodical because they lack any better quality. The prose of zombies is laundered sludge, and sounds like "Yours of the 7th inst. to hand".

The prose of conformists comprises, in any language, most of what is excellent and most of what is useful. It is the language of a good, practical cook book; it is the laguage of a good, practising journalist like Daniel Defoe; and it is the language of the greatest satirist in English, Jonathan Swift. In modern English prose, Graham Greene is a conformist, and so is Angus Wilson, and so is Frank O'Connor.

The prose of individualists comprises a tiny proportion of what is written in any language, and probably for the reason that individualists comprise a tiny proportion of the people in any country. An individualist's prose can be outré or ignorant or boring or goofy or vulgarly repulsive; but it can also be racy, thrilling, provocatively experimental and delightfully fresh. See the prose, sometimes, of D. H. Lawrence; see the prose, sometimes, of James Joyce; see the prose, often, of Dylan Thomas or e. e. cummings. See a good deal of the prose of Seán O'Casey.

O'Casey's style is sufficiently individual to invite parodies, you will there the individualists: Joyce Cary or Alan Paton or Edmund Wilson does not. However, if you look into any collection of parodies, you will find there the individualists, Wordsworth, Whitman, Henry James, William Faulkner. What is dangerous, of course, is individualistic prose in excess, even unnoticed self-parody; and that probably is the price such a writer has to pay for his eloquence.

For every noble paean, such as Whitman's on Lincoln, there is paired the ludicrous spectacle of Whitman admiring the smell of his armpits.

Of O'Casey's style, then, it must be said that it possesses liveliness and vividness in abundance, wit fairly often, and eloquence sometimes. It must also be said that it contains bad jokes and bad puns, that it can exude monotony and sluggishness, and that it can emphasise querulousness and bad temper. In sum, that the manner can easily slip into the mannerism.

Obviously, then, it must also be said that O'Casey's prose is not all of a piece. A simpler and, at his best, an ironic stylist like Hemingway could develop from the simple tightness of *The Sun Also Rises*, to the loose simplicities of *The Green Hills of Africa*, and into the elementary floridness of *For Whom the Bell Tolls* or *Across the River and Into the Trees*, and yet still be writing in basically the same style. Similarly, O'Casey could modulate from the eloquent opening pages of *I Knock at the Door* to the aridly jovial hectoring of much of his last essay, *The Bald Primaqueera*, and yet still be writing in pretty much the same style.

It was a style that did not so much develop as congeal. This hardening of its mannerism was derived, I think, partly from the increasing formulising of the dialogue in his plays, and partly from his rigidifying character, which, of course, happens to practically everyone as he ages. A man's character does not change violently with age, but its more dramatic characteristics appear in bolder relief, and the bolder dramatic characteristics of O'Casey's prose got even more bolder as he himself got older.

There are probably three main characteristics of style, any style — the quality of the sentence structure, the nature of the diction, and the choice of rhetorical devices. Of these three characteristics, I would guess that a controlled sentence structure is both the source of greatest strength and the sternest brake against dictional or rhetorical excess.

The mature prose of O'Casey probably first appeared in his disgruntled and irascible collection of theatrical criticism, *The Flying Wasp*. In that book, his vehemently phrased judgments of successful playwrights of the day, particularly Noel Coward, or of influential but foppish critics, particularly James Agate, are not so much wrong as they are excessive. His barrages hit their targets, but blitzkriegs are scarcely necessary to squash pismires. The only necessity for the vehemence was personal. The airy and witless trivialities of Coward held the stage; the intentional wit and intended profundities of O'Casey did not. Indeed, Coward was produced by C. B. Cochran who had produced *The Silver Tassie* but who had turned down *Within the Gates* while retaining his long association with Coward. James Agate had liked Coward and criticised O'Casey. So the angry resentment of the better man for the more successful one erupted from many pages of *The Flying Wasp* and caused O'Casey's publishers to advise him not to bring the book out. Yet he persisted, and Macmillan did bring it out, and it is about the liveliest, funniest volume of dramatic criticism to appear in English since Shaw.

Still, *The Flying Wasp* is not a superb book, mainly because the author's spleen is too pervasive and much too obvious. Its frequent excellence comes not so much from the author's feelings and opinions and certainly not from his embattled repetitions. It comes from a prose that is often so able, so controlled, and so wittily individual that the author's spleen is sometimes submerged and sometimes, in the sheer delight of writing, even abandoned.

See, for instance, the fable that takes up most of the chapter "Sainte-Beuve, Patron of Poor Playwriters, Pray for Us!" The fable is too long to quote here, but it begins:

> The Little Playwriters lived in the City of Dewymondroit. They were fed on dewberry dust and doughnuts specially made for them by the tribe of Criticonians who acted as the guardians in the daytime, and as their nurses at night. The Little Playwriters lived in dainty houses made of spun-glass, and where the sun shone these spun-glass houses were radiant with many colours so that each Little Playwriter looked like a little lizard encased deep in a diamond.

Here the creative distance necessary to write a pastiche in the style of a fable becomes such fun for the author, that fun wins out over spleen. Or, to take another example from the same book, consider the excellent effect of sentence structure and concluding alliteration in these remarks about Coward's play, *Design for Living*:

> . . . as if life would end because Gilda slept with Leo instead of Otto, and passing through a

The Silver Tassie
John Kavanagh as The Croucher in the 1972 Abbey Theatre production. (Photograph by Dermot Barry.)

period of four years, all the arguments, all the explaining away of the sun and moon and life and death, have been the screaming of Otto because Gilda went to bed with Leo, the screaming of Leo because Gilda went to bed with Otto, and the screaming of Ernest because Gilda decides to leave him, and return to her orbital movements from Leo to Otto and from Otto to Leo till the final curtain puts a veil over these poor wincing worms in a winecup.

Yet, fun as it often was, *The Flying Wasp* was of but minor importance; and the prose that was its glory required a bigger scope than the stage, a deeper tone than hectoring, and most especially a more humane theme. That bigger scope, that deeper tone, and that more humane theme, O'Casey found in the story of his life; and in it he wrote his most witty, vivid and eloquent prose.

The very opening sentence of volume one, *I Knock at the Door,* was evidence enough that here was prose stretched to a task both nobler and more demanding than any the author had ever attempted before. That opening sentence is about three pages long, stretches over eight paragraphs, and contains eight or nine hundred words. It is masterly.

Its structure has an overt and powerful simplicity of statement and emotion, laid over a complexity of form that is tense, tight and architectured. The form is so complex and so long that paragraphing is made to do duty as punctuation, and actually the paragraph break becomes a kind of super semi-colon. Yet the mortar of punctuation is never enough to hold a badly wrought sentence together. You can splash around commas and dashes galore, but, if you have written a mishmash of syntactically illogical clauses in awkwardly arbitrary lengths, no punctuation is potent enough to work. You cannot glue mush.

O'Casey's sentence is a consummate exploitation of

the parallelism of words, phrases and clauses, and the exploitation of periods stretched and stretched but never broken, and the exploitation of balances held and reversed and repeated and still held.

The sentence is too long to quote here, but its first paragraph introduces a woman in childbirth, and then quickly expands into a detailed panorama of the bustling late-Victorian city of Dublin, and then expands even more broadly into an evocation of the bustling late-Victorian world view. And then finally the passage contracts again in two more longish sentences to a view of the woman in childbirth, only now she is superimposed on both previous montages. The passage, then, has the fluid and economic swiftness of a film. This is how it concludes:

> And the woman in child-pain clenched her teeth, dug her knees home into the bed, became a tense living mass of agony and effort, sweated and panted, pressed and groaned, and pressed and pressed till a man child dropped from her womb down into the world; down into a world that was filled up with the needs, ambitions, desires, and ignorances of others, to be shoved aside, pressed back, beaten down by privileges carrying god-warrants of superiority because they had dropped down into the world a couple of hours earlier. The privileges were angry and irritable; but the round-bellied, waggle-headed, lanky-legged newborn latecomer kicked against the ambitions, needs, and desires of the others, cleared a patch of room for itself from the trampling feet and snapping hands around it; was washed, napkined, and fed; added on three, four, or five ounces of weight every week, taking most of it from his mother and a little from the life around it; and so grew gradually, and gathered to itself the power, the ignorance, the desire, and the ambition of man.

To me, writing such a passage would seem like moral calisthenics or aesthetic prayer. The necessity of creating, through a complicated sentence structure, a unique, appropriate and effective form can hobble the excess of spirits, temper rhetorical exuberance, and, if this does not seem too silly, even make the writer momentarily a better man. Conforming to form, whether philosophical or ecclesiastical or an aesthetic version of one's own creation can subordinate an individual's faults and quirks to the race's excellence.

However, even in this accomplished first passage of *I Knock at the Door,* there is a discernible overtone of O'Casey's most disturbing faults. Reading *The Flying Wasp,* one would have said that its author appeared as generally vital and vivid, but as frequently veering back and forth from the joyous to the discontented. These basic qualities also set the tone of the great biography. In its best passages, such as the opening, the discipline of sentence structure overtly and primarily engaged the author in the problem of creating an effective but complicated form and, therefore, imparted a control and contained his excess of feeling. In that first passage, dissatisfaction appears but does not overwhelm; it is held as a contributing part of the overall structure. Similarly, his vitality is restrained from exploding into mere bumptiousness, and his vividness held from descending into a pointless parade of gaudy devices.

With less restraint from structure, one of his major characteristics can take the centre of the stage. Then his legitimate critical dissatisfaction can turn into a disconcerting querulousness that hurts much of the autobiography in its later pages. Or it can turn into a vitality that finally becomes enervating because it is so long-winded and its content so repetitious.

The first volume of the autobiography appeared in 1939 and the last in 1954. In those years, there was some modification of the style, and I think that diction and devices of rhetoric became more important than sentence structure. Perhaps O'Casey was somewhat influenced by the plays he was writing at the time. Modern plays generally have few long speeches, and so there is less opportunity to do much that is complex or powerful with the sentence structure. In the later plays, the most notable characteristics of the language are diction and the use of certain rhetorical devices. In the prose of the later autobiographies and essays, diction and rhetorical devices seem also the paramount characteristics.

In the first passage of *I Knock at the Door,* there is a considerable range of diction. O'Casey goes from the colloquial "mucking about" to a literary phrase like *"tour de force"*. His references range from the universally recognised "Hollywood" to the moderately obscure "Aesculapius". His style ranges from the naïveté of a Beatrix Potter to a touch of Elizabethan rhodomontade. But everything is held in a tension never overstrained and never incongruous. Everything is fused by a tight control of the sentence structure.

When the restraint of sentence structure is relaxed, it is not only the author's personal characteristics, but also his use of diction and rhetorical devices that put matters askew. A chaste diction, such as we have seen above, can flower into floridness, and his favourite rhetorical devices can wax into just vices. Here, for instance, is the ending of the late essay "The Bald Primaqueera":

> Today I heard on the wireless of a fifteen-year-old lass diving into the sea to save a boy of ten. The boy was saved, she was lost. And of a policewoman who risked her life on a roof-ridge to save a baby which a half-mad father had in his arms, ready to jump off the roof, baby and all, had the brave woman not snatched it from the frantic father. Brave woman, brave teenager lass. Ah, to hell with the loutish lust of Primaqueera.

> There are still many red threads of courage, many golden threads of nobility woven into the tingling fibres of our common humanity. No one passes through life scatheless. The world has many sour noises, the body is an open target for many invisible enemies, all hurtful, some venomous, like the accursed virus which can bite deeply into flesh and mind. It is full of disappointments, and too many of us have to suffer the loss of a beloved child, a wound that aches bitterly till our time here ends. Yet, even so, each of us, one time or another, can ride a white horse, can have rings on our fingers and bells on our toes, and, if we keep our senses open to the scents, sounds, and sights all around us, we shall have music wherever we go.

This passage starts off simply and clearly, then veers into an ill-considered and rather garbled sentence, followed by a couple of fragments that are utterly O'Caseyan and utterly bad: "Brave woman, brave teenage lass. Ah, to hell with the loutish lust of Primaqueera." And then followed by a sentence whose diction stamps it as inimitably O'Casey's: "There are still many red threads of courage, many golden threads of nobility woven into the tingling fibres of our common humanity." But by this time the red and gold have faded because they have been pressed into service so often, and the fibres are not taut enough to tingle. However, the rest of the passage picks itself up, even despite the sad personal aside that does not belong, and concludes with a moving and memorable sentence.

In some of his later prose and plays, O'Casey writes too indulgently. His control wavers, and he tries to bludgeon through on pure personality, splattering alliteration and semi-puns about in a fine fury of ferocious frenzy, a merry melange of mingled-mangled metaphor, and a gorgeous galimaufry of glittering gaudiness. One wades through that stuff, knowing that he was too much an artist to be very bad for very long. But even his most tarnishable tinsel is thoroughly his, and the faults of his individualistic prose seem often more revealing than the qualities of his conventional colleagues.

He never wrote to hide or cheat. More often than not, he amused us with a brilliantly creative whimsy, and he moved us with a marvellously felt eloquence. And, as I remarked at the beginning, the style was the man.

'Self-portrait'
A pen-drawing by Seán O'Casey on a letter to Gabriel Fallon.

SEÁN O'CASEY'S JOURNEY INTO JOY

BRENDAN KENNELLY

There is an intriguing tendency common to some of the most interesting Irish writers. Looking at the artistic careers of these writers, we might describe this tendency as a journey into joy. Naturally, the different writers offer different manifestations of this tendency. What I have in mind is the transfiguration of experience, through language, into works of art, which, because their livingness derives from their attempt to understand and express the nature of suffering, become, in themselves, images of joy. One can, of course, use different words or terms to describe this transfiguration. Yeats called it "tragic joy". He also called it "gaiety"

> Gaiety transfiguring all that dread,
> All men have aimed at, found and lost;
> Black-out: heaven blazing into the head

Joyce's greatest work, *Ulysses,* ends with the most affirmative word in the English language. Yes. Yes to life. Yes, particularly, when so many have said no. And Patrick Kavanagh says that the true mark of a poet is his gaiety. So

> All true poems laugh inwardly
> Out of grief-born intensity
> Suffering soars in summer air.
> The millstone has become a star.

That, I believe, is what genuine art is all about. Millstones becoming stars. In Seán O'Casey's own words — "Life cannot believe in death . . . Though the purple of joy at times changes to a black hue of sorrow, there remain the crimson and gold bordering every horizon." O'Casey loved colour with all his heart; and his heart was the colour of hope. To him, the drama is a song of life, a song he never tired of singing. Let us look now at some of his encounters at different stages of his journey into joy.

Seán O'Casey was a proud man — fiercely, at times bitterly so. He was proud of his work, of his thought, of his politics, of his opinions. Most importantly, he was proud of the *humanity* of people. "Man" says O'Casey "is, at least, as kind, kindlier in fact, than God is preached to be, for man isn't responsible for most of the major disasters periodically afflicting the comfort and security of his own kind. Famine comes from God . . . His hand shakes a city or a town, and an earthquake levels the town or the city into a huge, tumble-down funeral pile . . . a bursting-out volcano buries a village . . . Pestilence, too, like the swift epidemic of 1919 that laid low in less than a year double the number of lives that were lost within four years of a bitter and bloody world-wide war . . . We have no reason whatever to be ashamed of our humanity; we have many good reasons to be proud of it."

Whatever one thinks of that passage, there is no doubting the emotional honesty of the man who wrote it. I wish to link the final joy of O'Casey's art with this belief in the value of people. I do not think that O'Casey is a very deep or a very subtle thinker. He is not an intellectual; he is a celebrant. The deepest impulse of the celebrant is to praise. Most of all, O'Casey celebrates people. Because his celebration is sincere, his criticism is often bitter. When he attacks modern writers such as Kafka, Eliot, Orwell, Huxley,

Genêt and Camus, it is because they are "clogged with a sense of sin, and frown upon any inclination of the heart to sing". How deeply or how superficially O'Casey understood these writers is hardly for me to say. I simply do not know. But I *do* know that he deplored what he called the "despairs of the American beats and the European wailers" and that this intense deploring of wailing despair is also a measure of his capacity for celebrating what he calls "the greatness of life; its stresses and its joys". I offer the following passage as an example of the impassioned meditation of a celebrant, that is, a man whose faith compels him to sing a song of praise.

> Man is the only life on earth that can see its form and love its grandeur; he has enriched the world, for without him it would have no meaning and look dead; it would be dead. He has ennobled the star we stand on; exceptional souls give things exceptional beauty. When Christ saw the lilies of the field, he said to those around him, "I say unto you that even Solomon in all his glory was not arrayed like one of these"; he gave the blossoms an eternal beauty; and when Shakespeare looking at another flower in an English field, said, "Daffodils that come before the swallow dares, and take the winds of March with beauty", he gave these flowers a loveliness and a courage unrecognised before.

It is the logic of O'Casey's celebration that, to him, the people *are* the theatre. One of his most fiery essays begins with that sentence. "The people are the theatre." And he continues:

> Nature sets the scene, and the man plays his part through the changing scenes of seed-time and harvest, in the cold days when the frost comes

> and the keen winds blow. It is from the things manifested in the people's life — their love, joy, hatred, malice, envy, generosity, passion, courage, and fear — that the truest playwrights weave their sombre and gay patterns of action and dialogue. Every art is rooted in the life of the people — what they see, do, how they hear, all they touch and taste; how they live, love, and go to the grave. The question for all artists is this: Is the colour and form of what has been taken from their life done well or done badly?

Before we accuse him of what O'Casey himself calls "Bolshevist blathering", let us see if this is true of O'Casey's work. To read through his plays — or better still to see them — is to become increasingly aware of O'Casey's reverence for life, his respect and affection for those who add to it, usually by their gaiety, and his savage scorn for those who diminish it, usually by their callous application of the heartless standards of mechanical moralities. There can be no doubt that when O'Casey says "The people are the theatre", he means precisely that.

Because of his faith in people, O'Casey was intensely critical of plays and poems which seemed to him to speak despairingly of humanity. He hit out angrily at what he considered was modern poetry's obsession with futility and despair. With a sort of baffled anger, O'Casey puts a question to modern poets.

> Where is the energy and the humanity in the poetry of our major poets today? Life with them seems to be either rushing to destruction like the Gadarene swine, or running headlong down a hill. 'The dream', as Auden says, 'always leads to the nightmare garden'; or as dull as 'Mrs. Dale's Diary'. As for being 'humane', or even

human, full of 'ordinary human feelings', there is not a touch of them in any poem, because they don't seem to know what ordinary human feelings are, or what they are like.

Then, with a quite irrepressible delight, O'Casey proceeds to give a poem of his own, called *It's No Go,* in which he used the rhythms of Louis MacNeice's *Bagpipe Music* to express his dislike of art that cannot rise above despair.

It's no go the gloom or the pessimistic bawl,
It's no go the death-cry, it's no go at all;
Life saunters jauntily, life always has her say,
Plays her games, has a dance, and wears her
ribbons gay.

It's no go the poet's round of ever-present doom,
For her laughter's heard in London streets and
in the Devon coombe.
It's no go the lesson teaching ev'ry step's a fall,
For life gets quick up on her feet, so it's no go
at all!

It's no go the chanting of the poet's Doomsday
Song,
That everything that's right becomes just every-
thing that's wrong;
For life can even sing of life twixt St. Peter and
St. Paul;
So it's no go thinking differ, it's no go at all(!).

O'Casey declares war on every resolutely pessimistic view of man. The play which best dramatises this war on despair is *Within The Gates*. In this play, O'Casey is campaigning for hope, battling away on behalf of youth and energy and colourful pleasure. He fights against the hopelessness of our age, the grey vague figures who go past in a slow, shuffling march, chanting their miserere. Here is the voice of modern despair.

> We challenge life no more, no more, with our
>   dead faith, and our dead hope;
> We carry furl'd the fainting flag of a dead hope
>   and a dead faith.
> Day sings no song, neither is there room for
>   rest beside night in her sleeping;
> We've but a sigh for a song, and a deep sigh
>   for a drum-beat.
> Oh where shall we go when the day calls?
> Oh where shall we sleep when the night falls?
> We've but a sigh for a song, and deep sigh for
>   a drum-beat!

Against the despairing multitudes, those who "challenge life no more", O'Casey puts the gaiety of the singer and the dancer. War is one of O'Casey's great themes; the deepest war is the war between life and death, between hope and despair. There is no doubt as to which side O'Casey belongs.

> Sing and dance, dance and sing,
> Brief life should be a joyous thing;
> The minds that are to troubles wed
> Are fit to host but with the dead!
> Sling out woe, hug joy instead . . .

I believe Seán O'Casey thought a great deal about happiness because he had seen so much misery. There is nothing facile or shallow or gaudily optimistic about his conviction that people have the right to be happy. He was not a man to ignore suffering and wretchedness, in whatever form they might appear. It is precisely because he had witnessed despair that his celebration of joy is convincing. Even as he watched his own son die, he praised the life of which that son was once a handsome and vital part. O'Casey never deliberately represses or distorts any feeling; he tends to give all his emotions the fullest expression possible, though he does so, on the whole, without indulgence. One reason why I think his plays will last is because they are, for the most part, emotionally real, emotionally credible. O'Casey himself is always emotionally honest as a writer, even when he is unjust or cockeyed. He obviously thought a great deal about feeling and was convinced of its primacy and importance in human life. He says:

> Feeling, rather than thought or detachment, seems to dominate the world of life. It was not thought but feeling that led the way to human development, for the meaning of the word is based on the word 'to grope', and life, in its first stage of withdrawal from the world's waters, must have felt, groped, its way in to the land. When hands grew handier, we groped our way forward more accurately, and, even today, with all our knowledge and our dependence on mind, the fingers retain an amazingly delicate sense of touch. We usually trust our feelings. How does one feel towards this or that? How often the question is asked! 'I felt sympathy towards him or her; I felt obliged to do that or this; I felt it was time to go; I feel something is bound to happen'; the examples of the use of feeling are a multitude, and there is no escape from them, even in a snarl of a poem or snarl of a play, for cynicism itself is prompted by the feeling that there is little or no hope in humanity.

The more a writer acknowledges the importance of feeling, the more *musical* his writing will tend to be. The musical potential of language is linked with the heart's capacity to admit emotion. There is a unique music in O'Casey — a music deriving from his determination to think as deeply and fairly as he could, of all those feelings, latent or vividly living within us, sometimes in a bewildering riot of contradiction, and of which we are all victims. The artist is an articulate victim. O'Casey always tried to impart this music of emotional complexity. He didn't always succeed; but he knew what he wanted to do. When he read Shakespeare, he saw it powerfully done. He said:

> Bitter, even savage as Shakespeare so often was, he never lost the lovely power of emotional compassion; nor, indeed, did the other Elizabethans, though they could be as realistic, as fierce, as dire, as any bitter and cynical writer of today; whose savagery, bitterness and cynicism is always sly, mean and commonplace; with the exception of Beckett who, alongside the greater Elizabethans, never loses the emotion of a great compassion. Ready for tears, as ready for laughter, how bitter Shakespeare can be when he is in the mood . . . And Shakespeare looked, saw life, and pronounced it good and lovely . . . Shakespeare does not stay very long with his sorrows; he sings and dances even in the midst of them.

These are O'Casey's words about Shakespeare; they could be applied, quite as fitly, to O'Casey's own work. How bitter he can be at times! How steeped in sorrows! But he sings and dances even in the midst of them.

A belief in people; a love and understanding of the dramatic portrayal of emotional complexity; a trust in the curative, even redemptive musicality of language; an awareness that even in moments of the most savage cynicism, compassion should be allowed its life; an adamant, agile refusal to dwell too long in sorrow — all these surely point to what is most vital in O'Casey. I mean his comic genius. Many attempts have been made to define comedy. If we are to appreciate O'Casey's journey into joy, we must try to define, or at least describe, what comedy is to this great-hearted artist. What are the sources of the seemingly inexhaustible energy of O'Casey's comedy?

It is O'Casey's belief that "Man's real fight has always been against sorrow of every kind, a fight to banish it out of sight, out of feeling, out of the earth altogether; to abolish the weariness of hard work, the sorrows of insufficient food, the misery of cold clothing, of misery-making homes, of the pains of illnesses, and, when possible, the unhappiness of death to life before life is ripe enough to discard the care of going". This was O'Casey's wish for humanity; it is the wish of an idealist; it is impossible. At any rate, it is impossible in life. Is it impossible in art, in drama? No. In drama, this ideal is made possible by the recogniton and presentation of men's selfishness, the one emotional commodity of which men have an inexhaustible supply, and by turning that selfishness into comedy. We can tolerate, even *admire* in art, persons, ideas, situations, feelings and attitudes that, in real life, would infuriate us, or even drive us mad. O'Casey himself was quick to recognise this. Speaking of his comic characters, such as Captain Boyle, O'Casey says that he loves them, "so long as I am independent of them, and amn't forced to live with them". Objectively for O'Casey, these characters "are always a nuisance to those who live with them, at times a menace, despoiling and ruining the lives of others (as per Captain Boyle), hindering and thwarting sense and sensibility".

Now, I think the question we have got to ask is this: why do we, the audience, get such a laughing, animating kick out of people who, in O'Casey's own words, are "a menace, despoiling and ruining the lives of others"? Further, and this is an even more intriguing question, why does O'Casey, whose idealistic wish for humanity smacks of a truly naïve goodness, present with such gusto and affection those characters who are committed to the destruction of O'Casey's ideal? If I begin to understand it, I think the answer lies in the amoral absolution of comedy.

To repeat and amplify the question: why do we *like* men such as Joxer and the Captain who are so useless, mean, treacherous and irresponsible? The wages of sin, we are told, are death. I suggest that the wages of laughter are pardon. Those who are part of the comic O'Casey scene are not condemned for their vices; they are appreciated because of them. O'Casey's comedy recognises that "virtuous" people can be very boring, and that "wicked" people can be very entertaining. The comic character, enjoying the insights of an amoral code of behaviour, knows that the only way to cope with the problem of hard work is to stop doing it; the best way to banish the "sorrows of insufficient food" is to guarantee a plentiful supply of drink; and the most effective way to avoid the "unhappiness of death to life before life is ripe enough to discard the care of going" is to live as if there were *no* death, by ensuring the endless gratification of all the senses, by an unfaltering devotion to the gods of comfort, and by the adamant assertion of the comic ideal itself — personal survival as a result of total emotional indifference to the sorrows and troubles of others. What I am describing now is an irresponsible monster — that monster which comedy drags out into the laughing light of day. And yet that monster is human; and he has the ability to spark a strange, sympathetic humanity in us. We are brought face to face with our own buried capacity for monstrous behaviour, and in one mesmeric side-splitting moment, we fall in love with our capacity for sin. The possibility exists that, in one more moment, we might begin to regret all the sins

Juno and the Paycock
Sara Allgood as Juno, F. J. McCormick as Joxer and Barry Fitzgerald as Captain Boyle in the first production, 11 March 1924. (Pen-drawing by Grace Plunkett.)

we have carefully failed to commit because we were too busy being "good". Under O'Casey's comic spell, we witness our own abhorrent selves in uninhibited action, and we rejoice in the momentary freedom of those irresponsibles whom we normally keep caged in our hearts, manacled in cells of respectability, as we work, pay income tax, dutifully remember to wash our teeth remembering the curious effect of bad breath on our colleagues, rear the children, and try to get on with or without the husband or wife.

That is a brief picture of the drab decencies on which comedy declares hilarious war. Comedy brings us in contact with the frightening possibilities of amoral freedom. Comedy *is* freedom — the freedom to be selfish and predatory. This contact which we permit ourselves to establish with the free, amoral, articulate images of our buried irresponsibility, even criminality, creates laughter of a very special kind and with a special energy. It is the laughter of one who has paid his money to be a spectator and then discovers that he is an accomplice. Tried, and found guilty, he is sentenced to laugh away his guilt in a place suddenly devoid of gloom, and electric with gaiety. We are now in the real presence of the comic figure, the full irresponsibility of whose anarchic being is an insult to the concept of duty, the idea of work, the notion of altruism, the chastening, changing power of suffering, the commitment to familial and social responsibility. The comic figure could not care less about anything, except his own sensual survival. And he survives because he is a predator. He lives because he feeds and drinks off others. His emotional immunity can be measured in terms of the suffering he causes to others. He endures because his are the resources of irresponsibility — lying, duplicity, cunning, idleness, deception, hypocrisy, treachery and, above all, the strength of selfishness. And yet we find a place for him in our hearts. O'Casey's comedy moves us to laughter and forgiveness. We forgive others. We forgive ourselves. But when we leave the theatre, we return to "civilized living", and to duty, work, decency and, most likely, to those private, steely attitudes of rational, responsible unforgiveness. In short, we are "moral" again.

I think it is a real sign of O'Casey's greatness as an artist than his foraging imagination could sympathise with what his humane vision abhorred. What makes his plays of lasting interest to me is this clear-eyed triumph of instinctive creative sympathy over impassioned political conviction. In his weaker plays, this process is reversed.

As a writer, O'Casey has many weaknesses. The worst of these is a kind of intellectual rant, a sort of isolated raving, most obvious in his *Autobiographies* where he is sometimes unjust to others and boring about himself. He is capable of tedium on an epic scale, writing at times like James Joyce parodying James Joyce parodying everybody else. But my overall impression of O'Casey is of a man, an artist who, in his proper medium, the drama, could present a varied, conflicting, credible picture of humanity at once trapped and exultant in a world of suffering, deprivation, sickness, violence and momentarily absolving and salving laughter. It is this great-hearted laughter of the instinctive lover and celebrant of humanity that endures. Near the end of his life, the end of his journey into joy, he was writing as he had always written at his best, writing as a man of hope in a world of apparent despair, as a man of faith in a world of sad unbelief. To the end, O'Casey cherished his hope and kept his faith. What more dare we ask of anyone?

> Even here, even now, when the sun had set and the evening star was chastely touching the bosom of the night, there were things to say, things to do. A drink first! What would he drink to — the past, the present, the future? To all of them! He

would drink to the life that embraced the three of them! Here, with whitened hair, desires failing, strength ebbing out of him, with the sun gone down, and with only the serenity and the calm warning of the evening star left to him, he drank to Life, to all it had been, to what it was, to what it would be. Hurrah!

THE ENIGMA OF SEÁN O'CASEY

A Summing-up by
MICHEÁL Ó hAODHA

In a span of theatre stretching from the social plays of Ibsen and Shaw to the Theatre of Cruelty and the Absurd, the playwright Seán O'Casey emerges as one of the last romantics in his art and his life. His writings illuminate his life which, in turn, is mirrored in his art.

His earliest experiences of theatre were in the melodramas of Boucicault and Whitbread at the Mechanics Institute and the Queen's Theatre. He was a protegée of the non-literary theatre and made his first appearance on stage with Frank D'Alton and Charlie Sullivan in the part of Father Dolan in *The Shaughraun*. His own life had many of the characteristics of melodrama. He was a Protestant who became a Fenian. In the Gaelic League and the Irish Republican Brotherhood, he learned the rhetoric of nationalism. In the Select Vestry of the Church of St. Barnabas he learned by heart the sonorous prose of the King James version of the Bible. It is quite likely that for a while he was even a member of an Orange Lodge. According to Joseph Holloway, the Samuel Pepys of the Irish theatre, he was expelled for taking part in a parade of the Irish National Foresters to Parnell's grave in Glasnevin. Holloway, at times, could be a garrulous bore but he is seldom inaccurate, and his version of the affair has been confirmed by O'Casey's old "buttie", Gabriel Fallon. O'Casey only states that he knew the Dublin Brethren well, a fact which is quite clear from his portrayal of Adolphus Grigson in *The Shadow of a*

Gunman. Ernest Blythe, a Northern Protestant, in his autobiography *Treasna na Bóinne* tells of O'Casey's High Church outlook among Low Church Orangemen. There were several among his near neighbours in the East Wall area who had come there from Belfast to work for the Great Northern Railway. It was O'Casey who swore Ernest Blythe into the I.R.B. and who initiated him into the intricacies of the game of hurling in the Phoenix Park. Piping with the Saint Laurence O'Toole's Pipers' Band was another O'Casey enthusiasm usually shunned by his co-religionists. The late Desmond Ryan in his book *Remembering Sion* gives this vivid description of an Irish revolutionary:

> Seán O'Casey sits in silence at the back of the hall during the lecture, a dour and fiery figure swathed in labourer's garb, for he works in the railways just then. His neck and throat are bound in the coils of a thick white muffler, and he looks a Jacobin of Jacobins as his small sharp and red-rimmed eyes stab all the beauty and sorrow of the world. He speaks first, and very fluently and eloquently in Irish, then launches out into a violent Republican oration in English, stark and forceful, Biblical in diction with gorgeous tints of rhetoric and bursts of anti-English Nationalism of the most uncompromising style.

But this enthusiasm for a separatist physical force movement gave way to a commitment to the cause of Labour during the Lock-Out of 1913; and so began his life-long devotion to James Larkin. O'Casey became Secretary of the Irish Citizen Army which later, under James Connolly, took part in the Insurrection of 1916. Larkin by then was in the United States and O'Casey had, a few years earlier, severed his connections with the Citizen Army on the grounds that Connolly had abandoned international socialism for Irish nationalism. Though not an active participant, O'Casey experienced much of the terror and violence of the War of Independence and the grim tragedies of the Irish Civil War. As soon as he resolved to become a playwright, he distanced himself from both nationalism and socialism. But he remained a republican in the Wolfe Tone tradition, not a pacifist, as some critics and scholars would have us believe.

Throughout the years, he clung to the mythology and rhetoric of what the older separatists called the Gaelic dawn. "The Irish are even a more scattered race than the Jews," wrote O'Casey in 1944, defending Ireland's neutrality during the Second World War. He continued: "We have knocked at every nation's door, looked in at every window, and sat down for a drink or two in the gardens of most of them — sometimes sword in hand that has helped the nation in whose garden we sat, to either plenty or peace, or to both; oftener with bales of lovely black, white, or red cloth, silver and gold ware of cunning workmanship, dressed leather, fit for the finest horses, frieze to keep shepherd and farmer warm, fine linen to lie cool on the soft skin of fair ladies, oak for the roofs of Westminster Hall and Whitehall Palace, huge wolfhounds fit to tackle a bear, and splendid horses as grand as the twelve of a beautiful white colour, with purple reins, dressed with silver, led in for the Pope's train. In the opulent city of Florence, the grandees, when a ship sailed in from Ireland, used to run races to the quay to be the first to get the noble stuffs that filled the belly of the vessel; all carried in an Irish barque whose oars, Claudian the poet says, churned the Irish sea into a mass of foam. All this was in answer, I suppose, to St. Patrick's prayer to God for:

> Gift of commerce from all parts
> Gift of ever-widening marts,
> Gift in church of reverent hearts,
> Bless stout Dublin town.

"The four first things," according to O'Casey: "commerce, fine markets, the grace of God, and stout in Dublin town."

This is history as written by A. M. Sullivan in *The Story of Ireland* or it might even be a quotation from Citizen Cusack in *Ulysses*. It also has some of the characteristics of Irish saga literature, an attempt to exhaust the details of an event or subject by a succession of descriptive adjectives. There is also the Dickensian expansiveness and ironic humour which gives grandeur and grandiloquence to Captain Boyle, Joxer Daly, Seumas Shields, Bessie Burgess and Maisie Madigan. It is this imaginative vitality which makes the early Abbey trilogy a compelling portrayal of the revolutionary period.

With blistering irony O'Casey exposes the excesses of extreme nationalism and the outworn shibboleths of the politicians. He draws on his first-hand experience of unionist, nationalist, republican and socialist parties and, with masterly detachment and compassion, reveals the basic conflicts. His language is a synthesis of the Dublin vernacular, Shakespeare and the Bible. In the longer speeches there are echoes of Synge's poetic prose. The voice is the voice of Dublin, but time and again, the dialogue has the colour, exuberance and the dying fall of some of the great speeches in *The Playboy of the Western World* or *Riders to the Sea*. But the prevailing mood is not pessimistic or defeatist but heroic, as far as his women characters are concerned. The courage of the women in face of the tragedies which overwhelm them is in sharp contrast to the equivocations of the men. But even the cowards are warm and human, and the brave only crave a home or a husband. Seumas Shields may be no Che Guevara but he claims to "have tarred a prayer for James Stephens' soul on the steps of the pro-Cathedral". He draws the line at the gunmen's boast that they are dying for the people, when its the people are dying for the gunmen. Even Fluther shows some spunk when danger threatens. But it is the devotion of the women which predominates. As Pearse said, it is they who keep all the great vigils.

Generally, O'Casey seems to take a critical or derisive view not only of working-class leaders like Connolly, who espoused nationalism, but of most of his associates in labour circles. It is not only the slum-dwellers who are wastrels. Every man's ideas and ideals are muddled and unreal; not a man would stick to his guns except Larkin, if we are to believe the autobiographies. Nearly everybody living is out-of-step except our Seán. A.E., Matt Talbot and Arthur Griffith are singled out for special condemnation. He was quite different where women were concerned. Only Countess Markievicz comes under the lash. This seems to be another instance of romantic ambivalence, that he was not capable of being fair to his own sex.

It is generally accepted that Donal Davoren in *The Shadow of a Gunman* is an outline sketch for a self-portrait. Davoren, the romantic poet who quotes from Shelley, is pleased to masquerade as a gunman on the run. But he is a coward at heart and lets a slum-girl, Minnie, who admires him, die to save him during a Black and Tan raid: "Oh, Donal Davoren, shame is your portion now till the silver cord is loosened and the golden bowl be broken. Oh Davoren, Donal Davoren, poet and poltroon, poltroon and poet." Is this a *cri-de-coeur* from O'Casey himself?

It would seem that O'Casey's failure to join forces with Connolly's Citizen Army and the militants of the I.R.B. who merged in 1916 had caused him greater anguish than he has revealed. In *Inishfallen, Fare Thee Well* he speaks of "the dark curtain of eternal separation" which the Insurrection drew between him and his best friends. In the long nights after curfew during the troubles, the ghost of James Connolly came knocking at the tenement door; that same rat-tat-tat which disturbed the love-making of Captain Jack Clitheroe in *The Plough and the Stars*. As Roger McHugh suggests in an essay on the *Politics of Young Seán*, O'Casey must have often pondered on what his fate would have been if, like the O'Rahilly, having helped to wind up the clock, he had come to hear it strike. Fortunately for Irish theatre, he lived to transmute this inner conflict and torment into art.

As late as 1918, he was writing articles and poems in praise of nationalist leaders like Thomas Ashe and in support of Sinn Féin policies. The old romantic nationalism blazed again as he wrote of the 1916 men who "fought and fell with the glow of burning buildings in their faces, and the glow of enthusiasm lighting their hearts in the effort to establish an Irish Republic." He sang that:

> Ireland's hour is striking now
> Sinn Féin's hand is at the plough.

But when he came to write *The Story of the Irish Citizen Army* in 1919, he tried for the first time to rationalise his non-combatant stance. He identifies more and more with Francis Sheehy-Skeffington, a true and sincere pacifist and non-combatant who was shot in 1916 by a trigger-happy British Officer. Sheehy-Skeffington, who tried to stop the fighting and looting during the Rising, is seen as the first martyr of Irish socialism, while James Connolly is relegated to a secondary place as a misguided socialist who succumbed to the pressure of middle-class nationalists. As C. Desmond Greaves pointed out in this series, it is an incomprehensible judgment on Connolly who had made clear his determination to start an insurrection. "Starting thus," he wrote, "Ireland may yet set the torch to an European conflagration that will not burn out until the last throne and the last capitalist bond and debenture will be shrivelled on the funeral pyre of the last war lord".

Another attempt to exorcise the ghost of Connolly can be seen in O'Casey's semi-autobiographical play, *Red Roses For Me,* where he draws on his experiences of the Railway Strike of 1911, and of the Lock-Out of 1913. The romantic hero, Ayamonn, is a young Protestant worker, a lover of Shakespeare and of a somewhat uninteresting Catholic girl. Clearly the character contains a great deal of O'Casey, as he would have liked to have been — a socialist martyr embroiled in sectarian conflict both as a worker and a lover. He accepts struggle, sacrifice and death in his altruistic desire to see a better life for the common man. He sees a shilling rise in pay "in the shape of a new world" and is prepared to die for it. The third act, set on the Liffey Quays, presents an apocalyptic vision of a new and beautiful city that the younger O'Casey saw in his dreams. The populace, transformed into ancient Celtic heroes, by Ayamonn's Sword of Light, chant a Hallelujah:

> We swear to release thee from hunger and hardship
> From things that are ugly and common and mean'
> The people together shall build a great city
> The finest and fairest that ever was seen.

It is an Apotheosis of O'Casey that Yeats had never dreamed of, a Blake-like vision of a New Jerusalem among the Fair Hills of Holy Ireland.

O'Casey's socialism only became explicit when he forsook the political arena to transmute his revolutionary ardour into those three masterpieces of dramatic art, the Abbey trilogy on which his international reputation is firmly based. The disturbances which took place in the Abbey Theatre on the fourth night of *The Plough and the Stars* in 1926 provided good publicity and ensured packed houses for the play.

O'Casey could have ignored without any loss of dignity the backstage jealousies and alleged intrigues against him by the Abbey producer and cast. But the attacks on his masterpiece by his fellow writers and the doubts cast on his integrity in the *Irish Statesman* were, to a man of O'Casey's temperament, a Judas-like betrayal. The iron had entered into his soul and the scene was set for the tragic finale — the rejection of *The Silver Tassie.*

After the great success of *The Plough and the Stars,* O'Casey went to live in London where he married a charming musical-comedy actress, Eileen Carey Reynolds. Despite the shrill hysteria of a great part of *Inishfallen, Fare Thee Well,* the move to London seems to have been a fairly happy and pleasant parting of the ways. He moved in the best circles and for the first time in his life he seemed safe from the begrudgers.

Most Abbey playgoers, who were almost all on his side, would have liked him to continue in his old vein as an ironic observer of Irish hypocrisies and failings. But, in leaving Dublin, O'Casey left behind his Dublin subjects to tackle a play on the First World War. It was a partial but conscious breakaway from his earlier Abbey successes. The first act is set in Dublin and is mainly realistic in treatment. The second — expressionistic — act takes place near the battlefront in France, in a lacerated ruin of what was once a monastery. In a series of short expressionistic scenes, showing the influence of Georg Kaiser and Ernst Toller, we see and hear soldiers chant and pray — not before a nearby Crucifix but before a big Howitzer gun. *The Silver Tassie* had been filled to the brim with gall and Yeats declined to drink. The great poet had little feeling for German expressionism and was largely out-of-touch with contemporary theatre. His last experiments with Gordon Craig screens and verse plays in the Japanese Noh style had ended in frustration at a negative response by Abbey players and playgoers.

Yeats and the Abbey directors should have accepted the play as Shaw said "as an act of God". The final decision might well have been left to the Dublin audiences, who had been so right about O'Casey's plays in the past. A few years earlier the Abbey had accepted and staged *Nannie's Night Out*, not as the work of an apprentice playwright, but as the fourth play of a successful and established playwright. It was a dismal flop but O'Casey manfully abided by the verdict and later dismissed the work as 'rather negligible'. If Lennox Robinson and the Abbey Company did not feel equal just then to the challenge *The Silver Tassie* presented, they might have engaged Hilton Edwards as producer or do as they did in the case of *The Old Lady Says 'No'*, in the following year, when they gave a small grant to the Dublin Gate Theatre to stage Denis Johnston's fine expressionistic play at the Peacock Theatre next door. If the style of production required for *The Old Lady* was outside the range of any Abbey producer in 1929, the position was most unlikely to have been any better when *The Silver Tassie* was submitted a year earlier. Apart from the artistic merit, the rejection of *The Silver Tassie* was a major psychological blunder from which neither O'Casey nor the Abbey ever quite recovered.

O'Casey's confidence was undermined in his capacity to handle a large theme in an unconventional dramatic form. His London rhapsody in Hyde Park entitled *Within the Gates*, again on an expressionist note, did little to reassure the playwright or his admirers.

The rejection of *The Silver Tassie* had confirmed all O'Casey's worst suspicions of Senator Yeats and the Ireland of the late Twenties. His socialist stance against the excesses of nationalism seemed justified as the romantic idealism of the fight for freedom became somewhat tarnished by the hard realities of the hungry Thirties in Ireland. A harsh literary censorship,

The Silver Tassie

Cartoon by O'Casey of Yeats, Lady Gregory, Lennox Robinson and himself on the rejection of *The Silver Tassie* by the Abbey Theatre.

Yeats: We decree that thou art a heretic.
Robbie: Cast out from the unity of the Abbey.
Yeats: Sundered from his body.
Robbie: Segregated and abandoned for evermore.
Lady Gregory: Amen.

although it did not apply to the stage, created a climate of repression not conducive to the free expression of ideas. The prevailing note was one of cynicism and disillusion. Yeats, still a father figure, began to flirt with a crypto-fascist movement, the Blueshirts. He even wanted the Abbey Theatre to stage *Coriolanus,* in modern dress, Italian style, as a parable for the times. Ernest Blythe, whom W. B. Yeats had appointed to the Abbey Board, had also been a member of the Blueshirts. The emergence of a bourgeois country, in which Church and State went hand-in-hand, was regarded by O'Casey as the final betrayal. It was in a mood of disillusion that he wrote such plays as *The Star Turns Red,* which is unashamedly propagandist. In it he looks eastward to Soviet Russia, not westward to the Land of the Blest, for the dawning of freedom's day. The setting is a city like Dublin sometime after the outbreak of the Spanish Civil War, where Fascism is crushed by the Red Guards of militant Labour. When it was published in 1940, George Jean Nathan, a lifelong admirer of O'Casey, commented that Communism had now adversely affected Seán O'Casey as a dramatic artist. Stephen Spender was also of the opinion that O'Casey's zeal for party line propaganda had perverted his artistic vision.

At best or at worst, according to one's point of view, O'Casey's later work portrays a somewhat romantic view of Communism. Red Jim, of *The Star Turns Red,* a more than life-size model of Jim Larkin, is transplanted from 1913 to the mid-Thirties, the heyday of leftist theatre in England. Even the tentative pacifism of the earlier Dublin plays has been abandoned. O'Casey now seems to accept that social revolution brings sacrifice, even if it means the death of thousands as a necessary step towards a socialist goal.

Nevertheless, a modern Marxist or Maoist would find the poetic humanism of O'Casey hard to accept. O'Killigain in *Purple Dust,* Father Domineer in

Cock-a-Doodle-Dandy and the Loreleens and Foorawns of a puritan Ireland are throw-backs, not only to the melodrama of the nineteenth century but to the morality plays of late medieval times. The genius of O'Casey is baroque and romantic; it belongs to the more spacious days of theatre. His verbal splendour needs full orchestration, not an arrangement for strings. His rapscallions and rogues are creations on a grand scale. Tomás Mac Anna, who has done most to explore the possibilities of these later works on stage in the New Abbey, has come up with an interesting and intriguing description when he talks of O'Casey's toy theatre, something of inexhaustible delight, not so much penny plain as tuppence coloured. But there remains the problem that in a toy theatre the characters are at best two dimensional and predictable like those in a mumming play.

Some critics have now come to accept the autobiographies as O'Casey's *apologia pro vita sua* rather than a factual account of his life and times. Many of the literary and political judgments in these works are wayward, if not downright unfair. In six volumes, Seán O'Casey assiduously presents a romantic image of Johnny Casside as a misunderstood artist suffering poverty and deprivation of the worst kind. This, as we now know, is something less than the whole truth. O'Casey was born into a lower middle class Protestant family. In later years, he certainly suffered poverty through illness and unemployment but it is difficult to understand, with his background and above average opportunities, why he was unable to get a better job than that of a labourer. There is some evidence of pilfering from his employers while in his teens but this is unimportant, like Shakespeare's deer stealing. Perhaps a clue to the enigma is that Johnny Casside bears as much relationship to the real O'Casey as Stephen Dedalus did to James Joyce.

Broadcasting from RTÉ over twenty-five years ago

to introduce a season of his plays on radio, O'Casey spoke of his work as "a tale told to life herself". A tale told to life herself is what O'Casey has left us in over twenty books and plays. And this tale must always have a meaning, for it was written sometimes with rancour, sometimes with humour, by one of the great dramatists of this century. Some of the wild joy and savage bitterness will, as he once said, go down into the limbo of forgotten things, but much is certain to survive as an incomparable portrayal of Ireland in revolution.

THE THOMAS DAVIS LECTURES

Series published by THE MERCIER PRESS

Social Life in Ireland 1800-45
edited by R. B. McDowell
Seven Centuries of Irish Learning
edited by Brian Ó Cuiv
Early Irish Society
edited by Myles Dillon
Irish Sagas
edited by Myles Dillon
The Irish at War
edited by G. A. Hayes McCoy
The Celts
edited by Joseph Raftery
The Integrity of Yeats
edited by Denis Donoghue
The Yeats We Knew
edited by Francis MacManus
Early Irish Poetry
edited by James Carney
Leaders and Workers
edited by J. W. Boyle
The Years of the Great Test (Ireland 1927/37)
edited by Francis MacManus
The Fenian Movement
edited by T. W. Moody
Swift Revisited
edited by Denis Donoghue
The Formation of the Irish Economy
edited by L. M. Cullen
The Gaelic League Idea
edited by Seán Ó Tuama

Irish Poets in English
edited by Seán Lucy
The English Language in Ireland
edited by Diarmaid Ó Muirithe
Trade Unions and Change in Irish Society
edited by Donal Nevin
The O'Casey Enigma
edited by Micheál Ó hAodha